The Six Wives of Henry VIII

A classic account of the rise and fall
of queens in the House of Tudor

by

Charles Twain

The Six Wives of Henry VIII

Layout and Cover Copyright ©2010
All Rights Reserved
Printed in the USA

Published by ReadaClassic.com

ISBN#: 978-1-61104-251-1

Table of Contents

1. KATHARINE OF ARRAGON

KATHARINE of Arragon was born when her native land was at the very height of its prosperity. Her parents were Ferdinand and Isabella, the powerful and popular sovereigns, who had conquered nearly the whole of Spain.

Katharine's early infancy was passed in a camp where Queen Isabella resided with her young family while her army besieged the town of Granada. This siege lasted for several years, but the town was taken at last; and when Katharine was four years old she accompanied her parents in their grand triumphal entry into Granada, where she lived until she went to England.

Her residence was in the Alhambra, that gorgeous palace, once the abode of the Moorish kings, always an object of wonder and admiration, even to this very day when it is' almost in ruins. Part of her time was passed in the cool, shady bowers of the Generalife, the fairy palace which stood on a mountain high above the Alhambra, in the midst of luxuriant groves, fruit, flowers, arbors and hedges, such as only a southern climate can produce. It was from this home that Katharine took her device of the pomegranate, which was used during her reign in England as a decoration. This fruit was once a production of Granada, and was worked on the coat-of-arms of the Moorish kings.

Queen Isabella was the most learned princess of her time in Europe, and knew the importance of a good education for her four daughters. Consequently she provided them with the very best tutors she could find, and they early became excellent Latin scholars. Katharine read the Scriptures in that tongue, and throughout her whole life continued to study it.

4

KATHARINE OF ARRAGON.

When she was sixteen years old Henry VII. of England sent ambassadors to Spain to demand her hand in marriage for his son, Prince Arthur. The union was agreed upon, and Katharine sailed with four young ladies and other attendants for Plymouth, where she was received by a crowd of nobility and gentry, who entertained her all the time she was amongst them with a variety of sports peculiar to their country. As soon as her arrival was known the king sent Lord Brook, steward of the royal palace, to provide everything for her comfort. The

Duchess of Norfolk and the Earl of Surrey went to meet her also, and the former remained as her companion.

The following month the king himself set out for Plymouth, but the roads were in such a wet, muddy condition that it was several days before he reached East Hampstead, where he met Prince Arthur, who did not until then know of the arrival of his bride. Next morning they continued their journey, but had not gone far when they were met by a party of Spanish cavaliers on horseback, who stopped them, and in a most solemn manner informed them that they could not proceed further, because their Moorish customs forbade the royal bridegroom or his father to look upon the face of the bride until she stood at the altar.

King Henry was amazed. He was quite willing to observe all reasonable forms and ceremonies, but to his English ideas this seemed thoroughly absurd, and he was not willing to turn back.

He had come to a dead halt in the drenching rain on that cold November morning, and felt rather cross at having his progress thus interrupted. After a few moments consideration he called his counselors about him, and asked what he should do. A long discussion ensued, and the conclusion was, "that the Spanish infanta, being now in the heart of this realm, of which King Henry was master, he might look at her if he liked." This suited the king precisely, and, leaving his son behind, he rode rapidly forward to the next town, where Katharine had arrived only a couple of hours before. Her retinue were thrown into a terrible state of perplexity when Henry made a request to see her, and presented himself for that purpose at the very door of her apartments. An archbishop, a bishop, and a count stood guard, and informed the king "that the lady infanta had retired to her chamber." But the more opposition he met with the more his curiosity was aroused, and the more determined was he to see the bride. He declared that "if she were even in bed he meant to see and speak with her, for that was his mind and the whole intent of his coming."

There was nothing more to be said, and further opposition might have given serious offence to the monarch, therefore the infanta dressed herself and admitted him. The interview must have been rather unsatisfactory, because neither could speak the language of the other; however somebody must have interpreted what was said, for King Henry seemed much pleased.

He withdrew to change his damp garments, and within half an hour presented himself again at Katharine's door, this time with the prince, who had followed him. In the presence of several bishops and nobles the young people went through the ceremony of betrothal, which was done in Latin, and therefore understood by both. After supper the king and Prince Arthur returned to the infanta's apartments, where the evening was passed in music and dancing, interspersed with singing by the minstrels. Prince Arthur could not join in the Spanish dances, but he knew the English ones, and went through the figures with one of the ladies of his own country.

Katharine continued her journey next day, and on her arrival at Kingston was met by the Duke of Buckingham on horseback, the Earl of Kent, Lord Henry Stafford, the Abbot of Bury, and four hundred dukes and gentlemen,, in the Stafford livery of scarlet and black, who came to welcome her into the realm. She rested at that place all night, and was escorted to Kennington Palace next day by Buckingham and his train. There she stopped until the Spanish retinue, as well as all the nobility of England, could make the necessary preparations for her grand entry to London.

7

THE ALHAMBRA.

In the meantime King Henry went to meet his wife at Richmond, and to tell her what he thought of their new daughter-in-law. The royal couple then came down the Thames, in a barge, with a party of ladies to welcome the stranger.

Three days later the infanta entered the city by London Bridge, riding on a large mule, according to the Spanish custom. The Duke of York rode on her right and the pope's ambassador on her left. She had on a broad, round hat, the shape of those worn by cardinals, tied down at the sides with a scarf of gold lace. Under this hat was a closely fitting red cap, and her long dark hair streamed over her shoulders. Her four Spanish damsels followed on mules, each led by an English lady, dressed in cloth of gold and arrived on a small horse. After these came the whole grand procession, and all advanced to Bishop's Palace.

[A.D. 1501.] Four days later the marriage ceremony was performed at St. Paul's Cathedral, on a platform six feet high and large enough to hold eight persons. The bride, who never entirely gave up her Spanish style of dress, wore a closely-fitting cap of white silk, from which hung the Spanish mantilla, embroidered with gold, pearls and precious stones, that almost concealed her figure. Her body and sleeves were made very full, and she wore a large hoop under her skirts.

Prince Arthur was dressed in white satin. The Archbishop of Canterbury and nineteen bishops and abbots were present at the ceremony. The king and queen sat in a box that had been built for their use near the platform. After the ceremony the bride and bridegroom followed the churchmen to the high altar, where mass was celebrated. Standing in the great doorway of the cathedral, Prince Arthur endowed his bride with one-third of his property. The princess was then led by her brother-in-law, young Henry, to the Bishop's Palace of St. Paul's, where a banquet was spread. The newly-wedded couple were served on gold plate, ornamented with pearls and precious stones, valued at twenty thousand pounds.

LONDON BRIDGE.

The following week a grand tournament was held in the open space in front of Westminster Hall. There was a stage erected for the royal party. On the right entered the king and his lords; on the left, the queen, the bride, and their ladies, and took their seats on richly embroidered cushions, under a canopy draped with cloth of gold. The places, that were arranged one above another, in rows like those in a circus, to form an enormous circle, were so packed with people that only their heads could be seen. Presently loud blasts from the trumpets announced the arrival of the knights, who were borne into the arena under fanciful canopies. The Earl of Essex sat in a pavilion among trees, flowers, and rocks, with curious-looking animals climbing up the sides. A handsome young lady, fantastically dressed, stood on a green hill above the earl. The Marquis of Dorset appeared in a pavilion all draped in gold, wearing a complete suit of armor. Lord William Courtenay rode an enormous red dragon, led by a giant carrying a tree in his hands. There were twenty or thirty in all of these curiously-adorned knights, who marched around the arena to the delight of the audience, and then engaged in a tilt that caused many a bruise and scratch, but no serious damage to anybody. When evening came on the royal company withdrew to Westminster Hall. At the upper end was a dais with elevated seats for the king, queen, the bride and groom, and the king's mother. All the ladies sat on the left side and the gentlemen on the right, and the nobility, who were not engaged in the performance or ballets that followed, took their places on the king's side of the hall according to their rank. When a couple desired to dance between the entrances of the regular performers, the gentleman would advance to the front of the dais from his side, the ladj would do the same from hers, and after a few minutes' dancing return to their respective places. The first pageant was a full-rigged ship drawn in on wheels. The mariners performed their duties as though they were really at sea, and used only seafaring terms. Next came a castle all lighted up inside, eight young women appearing at the windows handsomely attired in the newest styles. At the top window of the castle sat a lady in Spanish costume representing Katharine of Arragon. The princess must have been amused when she saw her double, who sat up quite haughtily, while two gentlemen courted her and sought in every possible way to gain her favor. For a while she treated their attentions with disdain, but at last, as in all ballets, matters took a favorable turn; the ladies came out of the castle, were joined by the sailors from the ship, and the whole party danced a grand set of exceedingly pretty figures, and then disappeared into the castle again. This structure was drawn by marvelous gold and silver lions harnessed with massive gold chains. But we must explain what these beasts really were. In each one were two men, one in the fore and the other in the hind quarters, so completely hidden that nothing appeared of them but their legs, which were made to look like those of the real lions. Then Prince Arthur danced with his aunt, the Princess Cicely, Henry, Duke of

11

York, with his sister Margaret, and Katharine with one of her Spanish ladies. There was considerable difference in the two styles of dancing, for the English movements were quick and lively, while those of the Spanish were slow and stately, resembling a minuet. The king and queen were much pleased with these performances of their children, and watched them with a great deal of pride.

At a grand dinner given in Parliament Chamber on the following Sunday, Katharine distributed the prizes won in the tilt. To the Duke of Buckingham she gave a valuable diamond ; to the Marquis of Dorset, a superb ruby, and to the others, rings set with precious stones. A week later the court went to Richmond, where, after mass on the first Sunday, they all assembled in the gardens and played games of chess, backgammon, cards, and dice, while some Spaniards entertained them with tumbling and dancing. In the evening a huge rock was drawn by three sea-horses into the grand hall, where the ladies and gentlemen were assembled. On either side of the rock were mermaids made of shells, and inside of the figures were the sweet-voiced children who sang in the king's chapel. These could not be seen, but their harmony filled the air as the rock was drawn slowly through the whole length of the hall. When it reached the platform on which sat the royal family, a large number of white doves flew out, and live rabbits ran about the hall, causing great shouting and merriment. King Henry closed the entertainment by making rich gifts of plate to the lords and ladies from Spain, who then took leave of their princess, as they were going back home.

RECEPTION ROOM.

Q. E.—23

RICHMOND CHURCH.

Katharine looked very sad after they had left her, and the king observing this sent word for her and her ladies to join him in his library. There he showed them all the pretty English and Latin books that he thought would please them, laughed and chatted in a kind friendly manner with his daughter-in-law, and then asked her to select some jewels from a lot that he had ordered for her. After she had made her choice, he distributed the rest among her ladies, and so won Katharine's heart by his warm, affectionate treatment that she ceased to feel depressed in her English home.

A few months later the princess went with her husband to Wales, where they were to have a little court of their own similar to the one at Westminster. Katharine performed the journey on horseback, and when she felt fatigued she rested on a litter, borne between two horses. This was the only mode of travelling before turnpike roads were made.

The Prince and Princess of Wales made themselves very popular in their new home, but they did not stay there long, for

Arthur was taken suddenly ill, and died of the plague the following April, 1502, just six months after his marriage. [A.D. 1502.] The queen was sorely grieved at the sudden death of her eldest child, but she did not forget to sympathize with the young widow left alone in a strange land, the language of which had hardly become familiar to her ear. She sent for her immediately, and had her brought to London in a litter covered with black velvet and black cloth that must have looked very like a hearse, and settled her in a palace called Arragon House, where she spent part of her widowhood. Her marriage portion consisted of two hundred thousand crowns. Half the sum had been paid, and her parents being unwilling to pay the other half, requested that their daughter should be returned to them. But Henry VII wanted to get hold of the other half of his daughter-in-law's portion, he therefore proposed a marriage between her and his younger son Henry. This was accepted by the sovereigns of Spain, providing a dispensation from the pope could be obtained. This was necessary on account of the relationship.

Katharine seems to have been very unhappy at this time, and wrote her father that she had no desire to marry again, adding, " that she did not wish him to consider her tastes or wishes, but to act in all things as suited him best."

Such dutiful conduct excites our surprise when we consider that she was the principal person concerned. It seems quite natural that at the age of eighteen she should have objected to a union with a boy five years younger, even though he had not been so nearly related to her.

Notwithstanding her objections, two such diplomatists as King Ferdinand and Henry VII were pretty sure to arrange matters to suit themselves, and about a year after Katharine became a widow, she was betrothed to the young prince. Six years elapsed before the marriage was celebrated, during which period Henry VII died, and his son Henry ascended the throne. Immediately after this event he assured the Spanish ambassador

15

of his attachment to Katharine, saying that he loved her better than any other woman in the world.

There was a great deal of discussion among the churchmen on account of the relationship existing between Henry and Katharine, but at last all difficulties were overcome and they were married. A few days later the coronation took place at Westminster.

[A.D. 1510.] On this occasion the streets of London were as usual all decorated, and part of the way to the abbey was lined with young maidens dressed in pure white, bearing palms of white wax in their hands. They were attended by priests swinging silver censers as the king and queen passed by. Katharine was attired as a bride in white embroidered satin-, her dark hair fell in rich profusion down her back, and on her head she wore a crown set with rich jewels. She was seated in a litter covered with white cloth of gold, borne by two white horses, and was followed by all the noble ladies of England in little chariots. After the coronation a grand banquet was spread in Westminster Hall. The king and queen were served on an elevated platform at the upper end of the hall, while several ladies of high rank sat at Katharine's feet holding her pocket-handkerchief, table-napkin, fan and purse. At the end of a week the festivities came suddenly to an end on account of the death of the king's grandmother. Then a pestilence broke out in London, and the court removed to Richmond Place, where Henry planned all sorts of performances, parties and masquerades, in which he enjoyed taking part. Katharine did not care so much for that kind of diversion, for she was naturally quiet and studious, and felt more interested in practical employment.

At one of the Christmas festivals the king slyly left her side during the progress of a tournament, and returned in the disguise of a knight, astonishing all the company with the grace and skill of his tilting. The applause he received induced him to take part often in these exercises, and when he would present himself before his wife in different disguises she good-humoredly pretended to be very much mystified. Once he entered her room with several nobles dressed as Robin Hood and his men, and another time when the foreign ambassadors were invited to dine at court Henry conducted his wife to her throne, then suddenly disappeared, and in a few minutes returned with the Earl of Essex, both disguised as Turks, while other nobles followed him in Russian, Persian and Moorish costumes, the last having their faces blacked. The king's beautiful sister, Mary, with several of the court ladies, danced a ballet in mask, which amused Katharine very much, particularly as the princess was attired like an Ethiopian queen. In all the decorations used on these occasions the pomegranate was mingled with the roses of York and Lancaster, and the Tudor device of the hawthorn with its scarlet berries.

RICHMOND PALACE.

At the close of the year 1510 the queen had a little boy, and he was named Henry. The king was so much pleased at this event that a grand tournament was given to celebrate it. In the evening a nobleman came to inform the queen that there was a gold arbor full of ladies who had prepared something for her entertainment. Katharine answered very graciously "that both she and her ladies would be happy to behold them and their pastimes." Then a large curtain was drawn aside, and an arbor moved forward. It had posts and pillars covered with gold and twined with branches of hawthorn, roses and eglantine, all made of satin and silk, the colors of the different flowers. In the arbor were six beautiful young girls in white and green satin dresses, covered with the letters H. and K. knit together with gold lacing. Near the bower stood the king himself, with five lords dressed in purple satin, likewise covered with the gold letters H. and K. Then they all danced before Katharine, and while they were thus engaged a very different scene was going on at the other end of the hall. The golden arbor that the ladies left for the dance had been rolled back close to where a large crowd of Londoners had gathered to see the grand doings at court, as they always did in those days. They began to finger the ornaments, and finally to pluck them off until they had entirely stripped the bower. The chief steward tried to prevent this destruction, but not wishing to disturb the ballet by using violence he failed entirely. Meanwhile the king finished his performance, and feeling in an excellent humor at its success he called to the women in the crowd to come and help themselves to the golden letters from his dress and that of his company. Little did he imagine what would be the result of this order, for scarcely was it given than the whole assembly rushed forward like a mob, and seized not only on him but all his guests, helping themselves to every glittering ornament that was in sight

They even went so far as to take the jewels of the ladies, and to strip the king of most of his fine clothing. One of the gentlemen was left with nothing on but his flannels. It was amazing what a clean sweep was made in a few minutes of all the finery. At last the guards succeeded in clearing the hall without bloodshed, and the king laughing heartily handed his wife to the banquet in his own chamber, where the court sat down in their tattered condition, treating the whole scramble as a frolic. No doubt the young king had received a lesson by which he profited later. A few weeks after his birth the young prince died, much lamented by everybody at court.

The following year Henry invaded France in person, leaving the queen not only with the reins of government in her own hands, but making her besides captain of all his forces, with the assistance of five nobles. During the king's absence the Scots invaded his kingdom, but were repulsed. It is remarkable that two of the greatest victories gained over that nation were those of Neville's Cross and Flodden Field, both fought under the management of queens in the absence of their husbands.

After the battle at Neville's Cross Katharine went on a pilgrimage to Walsingham shrine, and returned just in time to welcome her husband, who took her by surprise at Richmond, where there was a most loving meeting between the royal couple. He had travelled through his realm in disguise, therefore the queen had not been informed that he was coming so soon.

[A.D. 1514.] Henry had been victorious in France, and the war ended there by the marriage of his beautiful young sister Mary and Louis XII. Anne Boleyn, who was then a young girl, went with the bride as her attendant.

Mary was in love with the Duke of Suffolk when she was forced into this marriage with the King of France. In less than three months the young husband died, and then the duke, who was sent to France to take care of the widow and her property, married her. Henry VIII was very angry at first at the sly way in which this love-affair had been managed, but Katharine made peace between the brother and sister, and invited the young couple to Greenwich Palace, where she entertained them with a grand festival.

On the first of May the king gave a party, which was conducted in this way: Katharine, with the young bride and all the court ladies, rode from the palace to Shooter's Hill, where the king, with the archers of his body-guard, met them, dressed

19

like Robin Hood and his outlaws, and begged that the royal party " would enter the good greenwood and see how outlaws lived."

Katharine graciously consented, and was led to a rustic bower, .covered with hawthorn boughs and spring flowers, where a fine breakfast of venison and other good things was laid out. This lodge in the wilderness delighted all the ladies, and a couple of hours were very pleasantly passed in eating and chatting. On their return to Greenwich they were met by a car, all decorated with natural flowers and ribbons, and drawn by five horses. Each horse was ridden by a fair damsel, dressed in gay colors, and in the car, amidst garlands of flowers, stood lady May, attended by the goddess Flora. As soon as the queen appeared at the foot of the hill these young girls began a hymn about the return of spring, and preceded the royal party all the way home, singing as they moved along.

[A.D. 1520.] Queen Katharine had two royal visitors at her palace. One was Queen Margaret, widow of James IV. of Scotland, who took refuge with Henry VIII. from the troubles in her own country; the other was her nephew, who afterwards became so illustrious as the Emperor Charles V. The latter spent several days with his aunt, who entertained him royally, then proceeded with the English Court to that congress with the King and Queen of France known on account of its splendor as the Field of the Cloth of Gold. At that meeting the carpet beneath Katharine's throne was all embroidered in pearls, and the decorations of the camp were of corresponding magnificence.

BEDROOM OF HENRY VIII, KNOLL CASTLE

At that time Katharine formed a warm friendship for Queen Claude of France, surnamed the Good, a lady of superior intellect and taste. Henry and King Francis also became very much attached to each other, though that did not prevent their fighting when an opportunity offered. When Charles V. parted from his Aunt Katharine she presented him with a beautiful English horse, and a saddlecloth, of gold tissue, bordered with precious stones. On his return home, he often spoke of Katharine's happiness in having married so grand a prince as Henry VIII.

While Queen Katharine was in power several improvements were made in England, particularly in the cultivation of fruit and flowers. During the wars some of the finest trees had disappeared entirely, but Katharine had them replanted, as well as salad, cabbage and carrots, which she imported for that purpose from the Holland.

An old rhyme says: —

"Hops and turkeys, carps and beer,
Came to England all in one year."

We cannot help wondering why hops were cultivated, because Henry VIII., who interfered in all the most trifling concerns of his subjects, forbade them to put hops in their ale. The turkeys were brought from North America by a lieutenant in Sebastian Cabot's voyage of discovery.

Before giving an account of Katharine's wrongs and sufferings, which began after she had been married about ten years, let us see how both she and King Henry VIII. are described by people who lived in their time,

Sebastiano Giustiniani, an Italian who lived in England, says, writing in 1519: —

"His majesty is about twenty-nine years of age, as handsome as nature could form him, — handsomer by far than the King of France. He is exceedingly fair, and as well-proportioned as possible. When he heard that the King of France wore a beard he allowed his to grow also, which, being somewhat red, has the appearance of being of gold. He is an excellent musician and composer, an admirable horseman and wrestler. He possesses a good knowledge of the French, Latin, and Spanish - languages, and is very devout. On the days when he goes hunting he hears mass three times, but on other days as often as five times. He has vesper service every day in the queen's chamber. He is uncommonly fond of the chase, and every time he attends one he tires out eight or ten horses, stationed at different places where he proposes to stop. When one is fatigued he mounts another, and by the time he returns home they are all used up. He takes great delight in bowling, and it is the pleasantest sight in the world to see him engaged in this exercise with his fair skin covered with a beautifully fine shirt. Affable and benign, he offends none, and has often said to his ambassadors that he wished everyone were as content with his condition as he was."

Katharine was then about thirty-four, but looked no older than her husband, because he was a robust, burly man, while she had a slender, stately figure. Her face was oval, features regular, with a sweet, calm look, though rather heavy. Her forehead was unusually high, and she had large, dark eyes, and a bright brunette complexion. She usually wore a five-cornered cap, bordered with rich gems, that stood up around her head like a crown, and came down the sides of her face, covering the ears. From this cap hung the black Spanish mantilla, and around her throat, waist and wrists were clusters of rubies, linked together with strings of pearls, pendants of the same from the belt, reaching almost to her feet. In one of her portraits she is represented in a robe of dark-blue velvet, with a long train, bordered with sable fur, straight sleeves, with ruffles around the hand, loose hanging sleeves over them, and a petticoat of gold-colored satin, that shows beneath the velvet dress, raised on one side.

Katharine was very pious, self-denying, and almost a nun in her performance of religious duties. She would rise at different times of the night for prayers, and always dressed for the day at five o'clock in the morning. She wore the habit of the St. Francis order of nuns beneath her royal robes, and unlike the ladies of the present day, she was often heard to say that she considered no part of her time so much wasted as that passed in dressing and adorning herself.

She fasted on Fridays and Saturdays and on all the saints' days, confessed every week, and received the Eucharist every Sunday. For two hours after dinner one of her attendants read books on religion to her.

Notwithstanding this devotion Katharine enjoyed lively conversation, and often invited Sir Thomas More, whose society gave her great pleasure, to her private suppers with the king. She was fond of needle-work also, and left some rich specimens of her skill, that were for a long time preserved in the Tower.

Although she took great interest in all English customs, and tried to make her subjects forget that she was a foreigner, she never could fancy field-sports, though Henry expressed great displeasure because she would not mount a horse and hunt as Englishwomen did. For his sake she pretended to like games, though she really had little taste in that direction. Even after her misfortunes began, the great Erasmus said to Henry: " Your noble wife spends the time reading the sacred volume which other princesses occupy with cards and dice." That renowned scholar always held her up as an example to her sex, and dedicated a very important work to her, called " Christian Matrimony."

HOUSE OF SIR THOMAS MORE.

Cardinal Wolsey occupied a prominent position in England at this time, and he was a very good friend to Katharine until she felt compelled to express her opinion of a certain bad action of his, which was brought about in this way: One day the Duke of Buckingham was holding the basin for the king to wash his hands when the cardinal poked his in also. The duke became very indignant at such presumption, for he considered it beneath his dignity to perform such an office for anybody but his sovereign; he therefore flung the water all over the cardinal's feet, whereupon that worthy prelate scowled revengefully, and angrily threatened punishment. He carried it into effect, and succeeded in causing the execution of the duke on a charge of treasonable sorcery.

Buckingham had been one of Katharine's earliest friends in England, and she could not help remonstrating against the injustice of his sentence. She even pleaded for him with the king, but failed. Wolsey's opposition was too strong, so Katharine revenged herself by openly censuring his cruel conduct, for which he never forgave her.

The next year Charles V. visited his aunt again at Greenwich Palace. He came really for the purpose of urging the king to make war against France, though he pretended that it was to engage himself to his little cousin, Princess Mary, then only six years old.

Queen Katharine met him at the hall-door, with her daughter by her side, and blessed him as he kneeled down before her. He stayed in England six weeks, and the result of his visit was more fighting in France.

Then Anne Boleyn returned home, and was appointed maid of honor to Queen Katharine. She was a great beauty, and such a belle at court that unhappily Henry fell in love with her. But he did not make his feelings known just then because the queen's health was very bad, and no doubt he flattered himself that she might accommodate him by dying, and thus spare him the trouble of a divorce. However she grew better, and then, with Wolsey's assistance, Henry began to make plans for ridding himself of her. His first step was to complain to his confessor that his conscience troubled him for having married his brother's widow, but it seems strange that that inward monitor had been silent for so many years. He set spies to watch Katharine's actions, hoping, no doubt, that something might be discovered to help his cause; but he was disappointed, and the queen was secretly informed of his intentions. Q. E.— 24

Naturally she was very indignant, and wanted to consult her nephew, Charles V., as to what she ought to do. For that purpose she sent a faithful servant, but he was stopped on the way by one of Wolsey's agents.

She then expressed her intention of going to law about the matter, and consulted her confessor, hoping that it would be laid before the church. The poor, friendless woman might have known that she could scarcely look for justice in a land not her own against a popular sovereign and his all-powerful adviser. She had an interview with her husband, but he put her off with deceitful excuses and fair promises, and she was forced to await patiently whatever his pleasure might prompt.

In the meantime a pestilence broke out in London, and several of the royal household died of it. This so alarmed Henry that he made thirty-nine wills, confessed his sins every day, and passed most of his time in penitence and prayer, his only recreation being the mixing of medicines and the compounding of plasters and ointments. He even sent Anne Boleyn home to her relations. But no sooner did the pestilence disappear than his jovial spirits returned, and he began to write daily love-letters to his favorite. Wolsey, to aid the king's divorce, had made the pope believe that Katharine wished to retire from the world and lead a religious life, and it is possible that he thought she might be persuaded to do so.

[A.D. 1528.] She did not know of this deception until Campeggio, the pope's legate, arrived in England in 1528. Then, in order to disprove it, she adopted a different course of conduct, became gay and lively, and encouraged all sorts of diversions among her court ladies. She tried to make herself popular with her subjects, too, by being more gracious than before, and appearing oftener in public. This behavior was turned against her by the king's council, who were told that the queen was only gay because her husband was sad, and that she was conspiring for his death and that of his cardinal. Thereupon they advised Henry to separate himself from her entirely, and to remove the Princess Mary from her guardianship. This piece of malice was a sting bitterer than death.

Katharine knew that Wolsey was her chief persecutor, and did not hesitate to charge him with all her troubles as well as with being an enemy to her nephew, Charles V.

That emperor was very much distressed when he heard of the turn affairs had taken, and declared that if the pope decided against his aunt he would not complain, but if not, he would support her and her daughter as far as possible.

In May, 1 s 29, there was a solemn court held in the great hall of the palace at Blackfriars, Wolsey and Campeggio presiding. Each of the prelates was seated in a large chair, covered with rich tapestry, near a long table. On the right was a canopy with a massive chair for the king, and on the left a similar one for the queen. Henry did not appear at first, but

27

Katharine entered the hall, attended by four bishops and a train of court ladies, to say that she would only accept the decision of the pope, because the cardinals who were present were too prejudiced to be just. She then left.

After several weeks of discussion the king and queen were both summoned to appear in court. When the crier called : " Henry, King of England, come into court," he answered distinctly, and standing up beneath his canopy, spoke of the virtues of his wife and of his unwillingness to part from her, excepting to soothe the pangs of his conscience. Then Katharine was called. She was already present, seated in her chair, and merely rose to explain that the action of the court was illegal, stating reasons why such was the case.

Her name was called again. Then she rose a second time, and walked around the table the whole length of the court, until she came to where the king sat. Kneeling down before him, she made a most touching appeal, begging him to take compassion on her, a stranger in his land, and let her have some justice. She also requested him to suspend the trial until she could hear from her family in Spain and get their advice.

After she had finished her long address to the king, she made a low bow, and with a dignified air slowly marched out of court. As she moved away, her name was called several times, whereupon the person on whose arm she leaned said: " Madam, you are called back." "I hear it well enough," she replied; "but on—on—go you on, for this is no court wherein I can have justice."

Her appeal to the king had made such an impression on all present that he made a long speech, lamenting "that his conscience should urge the divorce of such a queen who had ever been a devoted wife, full of gentleness and virtue." The members of his council knew well that he was not speaking the truth, but they did not dare to tell him so. As Cardinal Wolsey was still a favorite, the king closed his harangue by an assurance that he was in no way to blame for the desired divorce.

A week later Katharine was summoned to court again, but refused to obey, and with her own hand wrote an appeal to the pope. The cardinals had done all they could think of to get the queen to consent to a divorce, and being at a loss how to proceed, they took a vacation of three months. At the expiration of that term the two cardinals went to Bridewell, and requested a private interview with Katharine. She received them courteously, impressed upon them her forlorn situation in a foreign land, deprived of counsel, and told them that she would be grateful if they would advise her how to act. She then withdrew with them to a private room, where they remained for nearly an hour in earnest conversation. She must have , argued her case well, for both the cardinals were won over to her side, and would never say another word against her. This was the only cause for offence that King Henry ever had against Wolsey, who ceased, from that moment, to be his favorite.

WOLSEY'S TOWER.

When the court met again, the king was very angry to hear that the question of his divorce must be referred to the pope. He wanted it settled in his way and in England. Shortly after, Wolsey had an interview with the king, which proved his last.

The king and queen passed Christmas together at Greenwich with the usual festivities, and seemed to be on very good terms, he treating the Princess Mary very tenderly, and showing Katharine the respect due the Queen of England.

Henry had an object in this; he wanted his wife to withdraw her appeal from Rome, and let the matter be decided in England, but she refused. Then he got angry, put a sudden stop to the court diversions, and retired to the palace at Whitehall that he had just taken from Wolsey.

Later, he sent a message to the queen entreating her to "quiet his conscience." She replied: "God grant my husband a quiet conscience, but I mean to abide by no decision excepting that of Rome."

This answer put the king in a perfect fury. After the festival of Trinity he accompanied the queen to Windsor, but left in a few days, and sent her word to be out of the castle before his return. "Go where I may," was the reply of the forsaken queen, "I am his wife, and for him I will pray!" She immediately left Windsor Castle, and never again beheld her husband or child. She went to reside at Ampthill, whence she wrote her daughter letters full of most excellent advice, always praying her to submit to her father's will. Her reason for this was that she wished the child to keep in the king's good graces, knowing that he would some time or other acknowledge her rights. Once, on hearing of Mary's illness, Katharine wrote to Cromwell for permission to see her, but was cruelly refused.

Finding at last that the decision at Rome was likely to be against him, the king induced Dr. Cranmer, who had just been made Archbishop of Canterbury, to conclude the long agitated question of the divorce by granting it. At the commencement of the following year he married Anne Boleyn, and there were insurrections raised in many parts of the kingdom on account of it.

Had Queen Katharine not been such a good woman she might have given the king a great deal of trouble by heading a party against him, particularly as the House of Commons had requested him to take her back. At the end of several months

Cranmer succeeded in getting the divorce settled; but the sorrow and anxiety that poor Katharine had suffered had broken down her health, so that when Lord Montjoy went to inform her that she was no longer Queen of England, but dowager Princess of Wales, he found her very ill in bed. She declared that she had been crowned and anointed queen, and would be called by that title as long as she lived, and no bribes or threats would move her in the least. She forbade her servants to take an oath to serve her as Princess of Wales, and many of them were obliged to quit her service because they would not disobey her. Those who remained were excused from taking the oath at all.

Katharine always judged her rival in the most charitable light, and seemed to think her an object of pity. Once when one of her women cursed Anne Boleyn, because she saw how troubled her mistress was, Katharine said: "Hold your peace! curse her not, but rather pray for her, for even now is the time fast coming when you shall have reason to pity her and lament her case."

Katharine had removed to Buckden, where she passed her time in praying and deeds of charity, or embroidering for the churches. After a while she regained her peace of mind, and made herself greatly beloved by the country people, who visited her frequently, and showed her the deepest respect. Other messengers were sent to her from Henry, requesting her to call herself Prince Arthur's widow, and to resign the title of queen. This made her very angry, and she declared that she was the king's wife, not his subject, and would be called queen until she died. She was the only person in the realm who dared to defy the king; she had lost his love, but not his esteem. Anybody at court who was known to speak in Katharine's favor was either locked up in the Tower or executed, and a perfect reign of terror was the result. When she heard how her friends had suffered on her account her health grew worse, and as she was anxious to live for the sake of her daughter she sent a

31

request to the king to appoint her a residence nearer London. He named Fotheringay Castle, a place that was notoriously unhealthy. But Katharine absolutely refused to go there,- and after a great deal of opposition on the part of the king's agents she was removed to Kimbolton Castle, deprived of many comforts that her ill-health made necessary for her. One serious cause of distress to Katharine was the imprisonment of hei two confessors, who, simply because they took sides with her, were subjected to the most cruel torments.

[A.D. 1536.] By the end of the year the queen was on her death-bed. When she knew her end was approaching she sent an entreaty to Henry that she might be permitted to see her child and give her a blessing. It was refused. A few days before she expired Katharine called one of her maids to her bedside and, dictated a farewell letter to the king, in which she pardons him for all the misery he has caused her, and prays that God may also pardon him. She commends their daughter Mary to his care, and begs him to be a good father to her. And in conclusion she requests marriage portions for her three maids, and a year's extra pay for all her other servants lest they should be unprovided for. Henry shed tears on reading the letter, and sent Eustachio, the Spanish ambassador, to attend Katharine's death-bed. He and Lady Willoughby, the friend and countrywoman of the queen, who hastened to her at the last, were the only persons present when she passed away. In her will she left a few legacies, but her income had been so cut down during the last few years of her existence that she had not much to dispose of. She mentions her dresses that Henry kept when she was so brutally turned away from his palace, and begs that they be used for church ornaments. She was buried at Peterborough Abbey, and for several years a canopy covered with a black velvet cloth, on which was embroidered a large silver cross and the Spanish coat-of-arms, stood over the grave.

Henry had a solemn service at Greenwich on the day of Katharine's burial, at which he appeared with his attendants in deep mourning, and commanded all his court to do the same. Anne Boleyn dressed herself and all her ladies in yellow instead, and heartlessly laughed over the death of the queen. "I am grieved," she said, "not because she is dead, but for the vaunting of the good end she made." She had reason to speak so, for nothing was talked of but the Christian death-bed of Katharine, and many books and papers were written in her praise.

A short time after her burial some of her friends ventured to suggest to the king that a monument ought to be erected to her memory. He answered: "That he would have to her memory one of the goodliest monuments in Christendom." This was the beautiful abbey church of Peterborough, for when Henry VIII. caused the destruction of all the convents and monasteries in England he spared that one because it contained Queen Katharine's remains. Through all her bitter trials no enemy was successful in tarnishing Katharine of Arragon's good name, but Shakespeare is the only writer who has properly appreciated her moral worth.

2. ANNE BOLEYN

Anne Boleyn was one of the beauties of the court of Katharine of Arragon, and was particularly attractive to the king on account of her wit and her fondness for pageants and masquerades, in which she took a leading part. Henry performed at these entertainments, also; thus these two were often thrown together, and the lady's vanity and ambition were flattered by the attentions he paid her.

She was an Englishwoman by birth, though of French descent on her father's side. Her mother died when she was only eleven years old, and she was taken charge of by a French governess called Simonette. She was carefully educated, and excelled in music and needlework. Besides, she wrote both French and English letters to her father when he was away, and that was an accomplishment very rare among ladies of the reign of Henry VIII.

[A. D. 1514-] It was probably on account of her superior knowledge that she was selected to go with the young Princess Mary to France when she married Louis XII., and her knowledge of the language must have been of great service to the young girl, who could speak only English. They had a very stormy voyage to Boulogne, and had to go ashore in little boats at the risk of their lives. It was rather trying to the Princess Mary and her four maids of honor to have to appear in their drenched garments before all the French nobles who had assembled on the beach to receive them. But they soon had a chance of showing off their beauty to advantage, for when within four miles of Abbeville they mounted white horses, and with thirty other ladies who joined the procession, rode into the town. Mary wore a superb embroidered robe, and her ladies' dresses were of crimson velvet, which must have been particularly becoming to the warm, brunette complexion and sparkling black eyes of Anne Boleyn.

ANNE BOLEYN.

When the King of France died, and Mary went back to England, Anne did not accompany her, but entered the service of Queen Claude, wife of Francis I.

This queen was a most excellent woman, and exercised a wholesome influence over her maids of honor. They went regularly with her to mass, attended her when she appeared in public, and spent part of every day in her society reading, embroidering, and weaving. The strict rules of this sober-minded queen were rather irksome to the lively English maid of honor, for she was fond of all sorts of games, music, and dancing, and is said to have invented many new figures and steps which she performed with much grace and agility. Another of her gifts was a remarkably sweet voice, both in singing and speaking. While at the French court her costume was a cap of velvet, trimmed in points, a little gold bell hanging from each point; a vest of the same material with silver stars, a jacket of watered silk with large hanging sleeves that almost concealed her hands, and a skirt to match. Her feet were encased in blue velvet slippers, with a strap across the instep, fastened with a diamond star. Her hair fell in ringlets about her shoulders. Of course she dressed in this manner only when she was very young; later, when she lived in England, her costumes were very different. She had one serious defect which, however, she managed to conceal with her long sleeves. It was a deformity of the little finger of the left hand which some chroniclers say was divided and formed two fingers.

[A.D. 1522.] She was about twenty years old when she returned to England and attached herself to the household of Katharine.

The maids of honor dined at mess in those days like officers of the army or navy of the present time, and were plentifully served with all the good food the markets afforded, besides an ample supply of ale and wine. Each maid of honor was allowed a servant and a spaniel, and those who were daughters of peers could have stabling for horses and carriages besides.

There was a young man at court named Lord Henry Percy, the eldest son of the Duke of Northumberland, whose duty it was to attend Cardinal Wolsey to the palace daily; but while that prelate held council with the king, Lord Henry would pass the time with the court ladies. The result of these visits was a love affair between him and the fair Anne Boleyn. But the king had made up his mind to marry the young maid of honor himself as soon as he could get a divorce from his wife, consequently he complained to the cardinal, and told him that he must break off the match at once, because he had planned a marriage for Anne with another person. The cardinal sent for Percy and took him to task for thinking to unite himself to anybody without first consulting his father and the king. The young man expressed his regret at having displeased the king, but declared that he could not give up his lady-love. Thereupon Wolsey swore that he should be forced to do so, adding: " I will send for your father out of the North, and he and we shall take this matter in hand; in the meantime I charge thee to go no more into her company to arouse the king's indignation." With these words he arose and went into his own room.

In answer to the king's summons the Earl of Northumberland did appear with as little delay as possible. He was an extremely proud, cold, narrow-minded man, who wanted his son to marry a woman at least his equal in rank and wealth; therefore at the conclusion of his secret interview with the cardinal he rated Percy soundly, and applied to him the most abusive and insulting names he could think of. He finished his long lecture by telling him that he did not mean to make him his heir, because he had other boys who, he trusted, would prove wiser men, and he would choose one of them for his successor.

Percy was then banished from court, and forced to marry Mary Talbot, a daughter of the Earl of Shrewsbury, with whom he was very unhappy. If only he had been strong enough to hold out in his love for Anne a little while longer he might have been spared a great deal of misery, for his father died in less than three years after his forced marriage, and he became Earl of Northumberland.

To punish Anne for loving Percy, the king banished her from court and sent her home to her father's house. She laid the whole blame on Wolsey, and was so angry with him as to declare she would be revenged on him. He could never gain favor with her after that. She lived at Hever Castle, with her father and stepmother, and was very unhappy on account of the great disappointment she had suffered.

After a time the king made an unexpected visit at the castle, but Anne pretended to be ill, and would not leave her room all the time he was there. But the tyrant was bound to have everything to suit himself, so he began to draw her family to court by giving them important offices, and advanced her father to the peerage under the title of Viscount Rochford. Still Anne did not return, and the king wrote her several letters urging her to do so. She dared not show him how angry she was because he had broken off her engagement with Percy, but she was treasuring up a store of vengeance against the cardinal, who had been his tool, that she hoped someday to visit upon his head. She had been away from court just four years when she returned, and Wolsey's enemies were glad to be able to count on her influence to crush him.

A short time after he was sent on an embassy to France, and it was during his absence that Anne gained a great deal of influence over the king. Ambition had entered her head, and seeing that Henry admired her, she determined to share his throne as soon as his wife could be got out of the way. He had asked her to marry him, and only awaited the settlement of the divorce, which was a long and tedious affair.

Anne Boleyn was soon living in Suffolk House, which the king had secured for her, and there she had a regular court of her own, with her ladies-in-waiting, her train-bearer, and her chaplains, quite independent of the queen.

The first introduction of Tindal's translation of the Scriptures was made while Anne was so powerful. Among her ladies was one called Mistress Gaynsford, who had a lover, also employed at Suffolk House, named George Zouch. One day the young lady was deeply interested in a book, from which she would not raise her eyes, even to speak to George, who tried several times to make her listen to him, At last he became very angry and snatched the book out of her hand. It proved to be the translation of Tindal, that had been privately presented by one of the Reformers to Anne Boleyn. Now, this work had been proscribed by Cardinal Wolsey, who was not in favor of any reforms in religion, and kept secret from the king. Mistress Gaynsford knew this perfectly well, and was so frightened at being discovered with it that she begged and implored her lover to return it to her, but merely to tease her, he ran off with it. The next time he went to the King's chapel, with the other courtiers, he took it into his head to read the identical book he had taken from his ladylove, and became so absorbed in it that the service was concluded without his knowing it. The dean of the chapel wondered what George could be reading with so much interest, and asked to have a look at the volume. As soon as he saw what it was he carried it to Cardinal Wolsey. Meantime, Anne had asked for it, and when she heard into whose hands it had fallen, she said: " Well, it shall be the dearest book that ever dean or cardinal detained." Then she went to the king, and not only succeeded-in persuading him to get the book back for her, but made him read it.

This beautiful favorite continued to hate Cardinal Wolsey more and more, and was determined that Henry should show him no favors if she could help it. Her mind was constantly busy laying plans to keep them apart, and to put the cardinal in an unfavorable light, though she used the most flattering terms both in speaking and writing to him. This deception she continued until he was won over to Queen Katharine's cause, when she declared her hostility openly, and she was a woman who would stop at nothing that would gratify her thirst for revenge. She was constantly poisoning the king's mind against him, yet the old friendship would crop out from time to time, and when the cardinal was seized with the pestilence Dr. Butts, the king's physician, was sent to attend him.

"Have you seen yonder man?" asked King Henry of the doctor. " Yes," was the reply; "and if you will have him dead, I warrant you that if he receive not some comfort from you he will be dead within four days."

"God forbid!" cried the king, "I would not lose him for twenty thousand pounds. I pray you go to him, and do you care for him."

"Then must your grace send him some comfortable message," said Dr. Butts.

"Tell him that I am not offended with him in my heart for anything, and bid him be of good comfort," returned the king, handing the doctor a ruby ring with his own image carved thereon, and requesting him to carry it to the patient. He desired Anne Boleyn to send some token of regard also, and she handed the doctor a gold tablet that hung at her side, adding a loving message, of which she did not mean a word. Wolsey raised himself in his bed when the presents were shown to him, and thanked the doctor joyfully for the comfort he had brought At the end of four days he was well again. But he was too near the court for the comfort or ease of his enemies, so the Duke of Norfolk, Anne's uncle, sent him word through Cromwell " that if he did not instantly depart for the north he would tear him with his teeth." He did go as far as Cawood, near York, but Anne never ceased her persecutions until she had him arrested for high treason, and employed her early lover Fercy to carry him the warrant. No doubt this was done to remind the cardinal of her first cause of hatred towards him. He was in prison only twenty-five days when he obtained his release.

HEVER CASTLE, BIRTHPLACE OF ANNE BOLEYN.

Q. E.—25

At this time the Duke of Norfolk, Anne's uncle, was president of the cabinet, while the Duke of Suffolk, her father, Sir Thomas More, Fitzwilliam, and Stephen Gardiner conducted the affairs of the realm, but she was the ruling power that influenced them all. She kept up her court with great splendor, and spent money most extravagantly. Still she could not marry the king until Cromwell's bold stroke that separated England from the power of the pope enabled her to do so.

WHITEHALL, WOLSEY'S PALACE, WHERE HENRY VIII. FIRST MET ANNE BOLEYN.

Then poor Queen Katharine was driven away from Windsor Castle, and the king created Anne Boleyn Marchioness of Pembroke, with a pension of .£1000 per annum. This ceremony was performed with great pomp. The king was seated on his throne in the presence chamber at Windsor, surrounded by his counselors and a number of peers. Anne Boleyn entered, followed by a long train of courtiers, and lords and ladies of the nobility. Lady Mary carried on her left arm a robe of state made of crimson velvet, lined and trimmed with ermine, and in her right hand a coronet of gold. Anne wore a jacket of red velvet with short sleeves, her hair hanging loosely about her shoulders. She curtsied three times before reaching the throne, then kneeled down at the king's feet. After that the charter was read aloud, and the king himself placed the mantle on the shoulders of the new marchioness and the coronet on her head. She thanked the sovereign humbly, and withdrew amidst the sounding of trumpets. Anne Boleyn's tastes were much more in harmony with those of the king than Katharine's had been, for she was fond of hunting and all games of cards and dice. She was a lucky gamester as a rule; but Henry's losses were perfectly enormous, and formed quite an important item in his private expenses.

ANNE BOLEYN'S CHAMBER AT HEVER CASTLE.

The exact time or place of the marriage between Henry VIII. and Anne Boleyn is not known. It was kept secret because it was so unpopular in England, but as soon as the ceremony was performed Viscount Rochford was sent to France to announce the event to Francis I. When the secret leaked out Cranmer publicly announced King Henry's divorce from Queen Katharine and his marriage to Anne Boleyn, who then began to appear in state.

[A.D. 1534.] Early in May, 1534, the king notified the lord-mayor that the coronation of Queen Anne would take place at Westminster on Whitsunday, and requested him to conduct her grace from Greenwich to the Tower by water a few days before. On the 19th of May the river Thames presented a most festive appearance. In obedience to the royal order a barge had been decorated and fitted up for Anne Boleyn's use in a most gorgeous style. The lord-mayor embarked in this, and fifty others followed in his train, one carrying a band of music, while the others were filled with all the great men of London dressed in scarlet, many of them wearing heavy gold chains about their necks, and others their order of knighthood. Hundreds of little row-boats were moving about on the water besides, for everyone who could procure any sort of a tug accompanied the chief of the city to Greenwich, or rested on their oars in the best positions they could find to get a sight of the new queen. On the deck of the royal barge was a tremendous dragon, surrounded by other monsters that were from time to time made to vomit forth fire by concealed artillerymen to the delight and terror of the different boats that floated near. On one barge sat a score of young ladies amidst festoons of red and white roses arranged on branches that formed a canopy, at the summit of which sat a white falcon crowned, holding a scepter in one foot, and Anne Boleyn's motto "Me and Mine" hanging on his breast. These young ladies sang the queen's praises in a chorus as they glided over the water. All the barges were fitted up with gay flags, flowers and banners. Having reached Greenwich Palace they anchored, the band performing different pieces of music, and the chorus of ladies singing until three o'clock, when Anne appeared superbly dressed and attended by her ladies. She entered her barge, and the gay flotilla moved down the river again amidst music, cheering, and the sounding of trumpets until it reached the Tower, when a marvelous peal of guns was shot off. The lord-chamberlain received the queen and conducted her to the king, who kissed her tenderly. The whole evening the barges hovered near the Tower, and from them was a display of brilliant fireworks, while crowds of people stood to witness them on the neighboring wharves and bridges.

How different were the feelings of the fair Anne within that self-same fortress only two short years later. On the eve of the coronation, according to the usual custom, the queen was conducted through the city of London in grand procession. All the streets through which she passed were decorated. The lord-mayor received her at the Tower gate. He wore a crimson velvet gown with a gold collar. First in the procession came the French ambassador with his retinue in blue and yellow velvet, then the judges, next the newly-made Knights of the Bath in violet gowns with hoods lined and trimmed with white fur. After them came the abbots, then the nobility and the bishops. The Archbishop of York rode with the ambassador of Venice, and Cranmer, Archbishop of Canterbury, with the French ambassador. Then followed two esquires wearing the coronet of Normandy and Aquitaine, the lord-mayor with his mace and garter, several more knights and nobles. Close behind them was an open litter drawn by two white horses led by footmen dressed in white damask. In this litter sat the bright object of the parade in a jacket of silver tissue, mantle of the same lined with ermine, her dark hair falling in pretty contrast over her shoulders. A band of precious stones encircled her head, and above her was held by four knights on foot a canopy covered with cloth of cold.

The master of the horse led the queen's own riding animal, bearing a rich side-saddle with trappings of cloth of gold that reached nearly to the ground. Seven ladies on horseback, dressed in crimson velvet, followed ; then came two chariots, in one of which sat the old Duchess of Norfolk with the Marchioness of Dorset, and in the other four ladies of the bed-chamber. Fourteen more ladies with their waiting maids came next, and the guard brought up the rear.

45

At Fenchurch street was a pageant of children dressed up to represent different kinds of merchants, who welcomed the queen both in French and English, the whole procession halting for that purpose. At a corner of another street was an enormous fountain that poured forth fine Rhenish wine all day long, of which anybody could drink just as much as he chose. One of the pageants was a white falcon similar to the one on the barge, with this difference: it sat uncrowned amidst red and white roses, and when the queen came opposite it, an angel flew down, accompanied by soft music, and placed a crown of gold on its head. A fountain of red wine flowed at another corner, and the three Graces stood above it on a throne, before which sat a poet who recited verses and presented the queen with appropriate gifts from Faith, Hope and Charity.

The city recorder handed the queen a purse containing a thousand marks in gold, which she graciously received with thanks. At Cheapside was a rich pageant from which proceeded music and singing, while Pallas, Venus, and Juno held up their apples of gold containing wisdom, riches, and felicity, which they presented to the queen. Over the gate of St. Paul's was a banner with this inscription in Latin: "Proceed, Queen Anne, and reign prosperously."

On a scaffold nearby were two hundred children, all beautifully dressed, who recited verses, and so after passing several other pageants and fountains of red and white wine, the queen arrived at Westminster. The palace was richly decorated within and without. She rode to the very middle of the hall, where she was assisted to alight from her litter, and led up the high dais, where she took her seat under the canopy of state. At her left side stood a cabinet with ten shelves filled with rich and costly cups and goblets of gold. After partaking of wine, cake, and sugar-plums, which were handed to her ladies also, she withdrew to change her dress, and probably to rest, for all the parading and sightseeing of the past several hours must have been rather fatiguing.

The next day was the one that Anne had looked forward to for many years; the one that was to place her on the throne of England. It was the 1ist of July, and at a little after eight o'clock on that bright summer morning she stood under her canopy of state in a purple velvet mantle lined with ermine, a band of rubies encircling her brow. There was the usual procession for such occasions, and the queen was conducted to the high altar in Westminster Abbey, where she prostrated herself while Cranmer recited part of the service. Then he anointed her on the head and breast, placed the crown on her head, and handed her the scepter, while the choir sang the Te Deum. She returned to her seat between the high altar and the choir, where she remained to the end of the mass, when her father led her to her private room off Westminster Hall to wait till the banquet was prepared. Then all the great earls stood in gorgeous attire prepared to wait on the queen in different capacities, the Duke of Suffolk as high steward, assisted by Lord William Howard, the Earl of Sussex as carver, the Earl of Arundel as chief butler, and so on.

When all was ready, the queen entered the hall with her canopy borne over her, washed her hands in the perfumed water poured over them by Sir Thomas Wyatt, and took her seat at the table, the Countesses of Oxford and Worcester standing on either side of her chair, while two gentlewomen sat at her feet. All the tables in the hall were beautifully laid and tastefully decorated, and there was music all through the meal. The king took no part in this ceremony at all, but remained shut up in the cloister of St. Stephen's a part of the abbey, whence he could overlook all the proceedings without being seen himself. During the dinner the Duke of Suffolk and Lord William Howard rode up and down the hall, laughing and chatting with the lords and ladies, and when it was over commanded them to remain in their places until the queen had washed her hands. She arose and stood in the middle of the hall, while the Earl of Sussex brought her some sweetmeats. Then the lord-mayor brought her a golden cup filled with wine. After she had drunk, she presented him the cup and walked towards the door of her room under her canopy. Before disappearing, she turned and presented the gold bells, canopy, and all its decorations to the barons who had carried it.

On the following day there were jousts before the king and queen in the tilt-yard. But the pope did not approve of this second marriage, and so expelled the royal couple from the church; and Henry's cousin Cardinal Pole, wrote him letters of reproach, calling Anne "Jezebel," "Sorceress," and many other horrible names. Nevertheless, the king treated her with all the dignity of her station, and had her initial A joined with his own on all the gold and silver coins that were struck after their marriage. Henry VIII. was the first and last monarch of England who ever paid his wife that compliment.

Sir Thomas More was one of Anne's special enemies, because he remained true in his friendship for Queen Katherine to the day of her death. When his daughter visited him in the Tower he asked her "how Queen Anne did? "

"Never better," she replied: "there is nothing else at court but dancing and sporting."

"Never better!" said he, "alas! Meg, alas! it pitieth me to think into what misery, poor soul, she will shortly come. These dances of hers will prove such dances that she will spurn our heads off like foot-balls, but it will not be long ere her head will dance the like dance." Her tragical end proves the truth of that poet's prophetic words.

When that great and good man was executed, the announcement of it was made to Henry while he happened to be playing cards with Anne. "Thou art the cause of this man's death," he cried, looking at her angrily, and rising from the table. He then shut himself up in his room, deeply grieved.

[A.D. 1533.] In 1533 Anne had a little daughter born, who afterwards became the renowned Queen Elizabeth. The opposition her marriage had met with from Rome caused Anne to side with the Reformation party, though she always continued a Catholic at heart, and observed all the ceremonies of that church. It is probable that she took no part in the cruelty that Henry exercised over the pious reformers, but it is certain that she made no effort to prevent it; for had she done so, she was still powerful enough to have succeeded. She had enjoyed one triumph after another, but when she reached the very summit of her greatness, no doubt she found that her path had been more thickly strewn with thorns than roses, and that in reading the Scriptures she felt the force of the text, which says: "What is a man profited if he gain the whole world and lose his own soul ?" She became grave and serious, and spent more time at needlework with her ladies, whom she assisted in making clothing which she distributed among the poor.

Probably this change was due to the influence of the reformer, Hugh Latimer, whom she rescued from prison, where he had been sent by the bishop of London; for it was after he preached to her and pointed out her duty that she so generously distributed alms and even paid for the education of promising lads who were likely to devote themselves to the church. She must often have felt that her position on the throne of England was not very secure, for as her capricious husband had behaved towards his first wife might he not behave towards her also?

HAMPTON COURT.

When the news of Katharine's death was brought to her she exclaimed: "Now I am indeed a queen!" But it was not long before she was suffering all the bitter pangs that the good queen over whose death she rejoiced had endured.

Henry had grown tired of her, and was carrying on a flirtation with the beautiful Jane Seymour, one of her attendants. And so, under one pretext or another, her friends were either beheaded or locked up in the Tower.

At last her turn came, and just as she had finished her dinner, on the 2d of May, the Duke of Norfolk, with Cromwell and other lords of the council entered, while Sir William Kingston, lieutenant of the Tower, stood in the doorway.

Anne asked "why they had come?" They replied: "That they came by the king's command to conduct her to the Tower, there to abide during his highness' pleasure."

"If it be his majesty's pleasure I am ready to obey," she said, going with them to her barge without waiting to make the least change in her garments. Arriving at the Tower, she was placed in the apartment she had occupied on the night before her coronation. Her attendants were two enemies, who were particularly disagreeable to her—Lady Boleyn and Mrs. Cosyns. These two women never left her, night or day, for they slept on a pallet at the foot of her bed, and reported every word she uttered. They made all sorts of impertinent remarks to her, and kept constantly annoying her with questions by which they hoped to prove something against her.

The poor queen was so affected by her close imprisonment that at times she seemed to have lost her reason. She wrote a touching letter to the king, appealing to his mercy, but he took not the slightest notice of it, and just one week after she was sent to prison a charge of high treason was made by the grand jury of Westminster against Anne Boleyn, her brother, and four of her best friends.

The friends were condemned to death, as almost everybody was in Henry VIII's reign who was brought to trial for high treason, though sometimes they were not even tried at all.

Twenty-six "lords' triers," from the body of nobles in England were selected to try Lord Rochford, Anne's brother; and, although he defended himself with great spirit and eloquence, and many of the judges sided with him, he was found guilty.

After his removal, Anne, Queen of England, was called into court by an usher.

She appeared immediately, and took her stand "with the true dignity of a queen, curtsying to her judges without any sign of fear."

The charges were read, and she pleaded "Not guilty," but the trial was continued for a long time, and ended by a verdict of guilty. It was her uncle, the Duke of Norfolk, who presided at this trial, and he pronounced her sentence. She was condemned to be burnt or beheaded, at the king's pleasure. Anne Boleyn heard this dreadful doom without changing color, but when her stern kinsman had ended, she clasped her hands and raising her eyes to Heaven exclaimed: "O Father! O

Creator! Thou who art the way the life, and the truth, knowest whether I have deserved this death."

She then turned to her judges and proclaimed her innocence of every charge made against her, closing her remarks with: " Think not I say this in the hope of prolonging my life. God has taught me how to die, and he will strengthen my faith. As for my brother and those others who are unjustly condemned, I would willingly suffer many deaths to deliver them ; but since I see it so pleases the king I shall willingly accompany them to death, with this assurance, that I shall lead an endless life with them in peace." With a composed air, she rose, made a parting salutation to her judges, and left the court.

The 19th of May was the day appointed for her execution, and the interval was passed in prayer and confession, receiving the sacraments of the church, and other preparations for death.

It was the king's pleasure that she should be beheaded in the grounds of the Tower, and that no strangers should be admitted. A headsman from Calais was brought over to do the horrible deed, because he was considered particularly expert. Anne Boleyn's fate had had no precedent in English history, for even in the Norman reigns of terror woman's life had been held sacred, and the most merciless of the Plantagenet sovereigns had been too manly to butcher ladies. But the age of chivalry was over, and Henry VIII was the first sovereign who sent queens and princesses to the block, without justice or mercy.

The unfortunate queen was duly informed of her fate; her mournful experience had shown her the vanity and vexation of flattery. Beauty, wealth, genius, pleasure, power, royalty, had all been hers, and whither had they led her?

She had not condescended to implore the mercy of the king, for she knew his pitiless nature too well even to attempt to touch his feelings. She passed the last night in prayer, and when morning came, and she heard that her execution was to be a few hours later than she expected, she said to Mr. Kingston: " I hear I shall not die afore noon, and I am very sorry, for I thought to be dead by this time, and past my pain."

Mr. Kingston told her that the pain would be little and very short.

"I have heard say," she replied, "that the executioner is very good, and I have a little neck," and she spanned it with her hands, laughing heartily as she did so.

[A.D. 1536.] Her last message to the king was : "Commend me to his majesty, and tell him he hath been ever constant in his career of advancing me ; from a private gentlewoman he made me a marchioness, from a marchioness a queen, and now he hath left no higher degree of honor he gives my innocency the crown of martyrdom."

A few minutes before twelve o'clock the massive doors of the Tower were thrown open, and the royal victim appeared in a robe of black damask with a deep white cape falling around her shoulders.

She looked very beautiful when she ascended the scaffold, with a calm and dignified air, and turning to Kingston she requested him not to hasten the signal of her death until she had spoken what she desired to say.

Then she began: "Good Christian people, I am come hither to die by the law, therefore I will speak nothing against it. I am come hither to accuse no man, but only to die, and to yield myself humbly unto the will of my lord the king. I pray God to save the king, and send him long to reign over you, for a gentler or more merciful prince there never was. If any person will meddle with my cause, I require them to judge the best. Thus I take my leave of the world and of you, and I heartily desire that you all will pray for me." She then removed her hat and collar, as well as the close cap from her head, and handed them to her ladies, who were weeping so bitterly that they could not aid her. Then turning to them she said: " And ye, my damsels, who ever showed yourselves so diligent in my service, and who are now to be present at my last hour and mortal agony, as in good fortune ye were faithful to me, so even in this my miserable death ye do not forsake me. And as I cannot reward you for your true service to me, I pray you take comfort for my loss. Forget me not, and be always faithful to the king's grace, and to her whom with happier fortune, ye may have as your queen and mistress. Esteem your honor far above your life, and in prayers forget not to pray for my soul."

Mary Wyatt, the sister of Sir Thomas Wyatt, the poet, who was one of Anne's devoted friends, attended her on the scaffold, and received her last gift, which was a little book of devotions bound in black enamel and gilt. She then whispered a few words to this lady, and kneeling down, placed her head upon the block. Time was allowed the poor unfortunate queen to say; "O Lord God, have pity on my soul," when the sword fell. With one stroke, the head of Anne Boleyn was severed from her body, and rolled in the dust.

There is a black marble monument in the ancient church of Horndon-on-the-Hill, in Essex, pointed out as the burial place of Anne Boleyn, but as it bears no name, no notice or inscription of any kind, there is no proof that her body lies there.

A great epic poet has beautifully said : —

"Tradition! oh, tradition! thou of the seraph tongue;
The ark that links two ages, the ancient and the young."

3. JANE SEYMOUR

JANE SEYMOUR has always been pronounced the most beautiful of all the wives of Henry VIII. But she has also been presented to the world as a meritorious, discreet, young woman. We cannot consider her so when we remember that within twenty-four hours after Anne Boleyn's head was cut off she became the king's wife. For it must have been while acting as maid of honor for that unhappy lady that she not only received the attentions of her fickle, heartless husband, but even made all the necessary arrangements for her marriage with him. We shudder at the thought of the preparations that must have been going forward for the wedding-feast at the palace, while the Tower was the scene of heart-rending agony to the queen, who was about to sacrifice her life for the gratification of a tyrant.

The giddiness of youth cannot be pleaded as apology for Jane Seymour's indecency, for she was no child when she permitted herself to be courted by the royal Bluebeard, and must have been entirely conscious of the enormity of her actions.

Perhaps her early education was at fault, but of that little is known excepting that it was acquired in France. She was maid of honor to Mary Tudor, queen of Louis XII., and went to England after her dismissal from the French court. Anne Boleyn occupied a similar position at the same time, therefore the two maids of honor probably knew each other intimately.

One day, after Anne Boleyn had ascended the throne, she observed a locket that hung from a pretty gold chain about the neck of Jane Seymour, and expressed a desire to see it closer. The maid of honor blushed, faltered, and drew back, whereupon the queen snatched the locket from her, opened it, and beheld the likeness of the king, her husband.

From that moment Anne Boleyn knew that her fate was sealed; she was indignant, but that availed her nothing. She found herself supplanted by a rival as she had supplanted her predecessor. Perhaps her punishment was deserved, but it does not justify the conduct of the king or his new lady-love.

[A.D. 1536.] When the axe made Henry VIII. a widower, Jane Seymour was at Wolf Hall, in Wiltshire, and her royal lover at Richmond Park. On the morning of the 19th of May his majesty stood under a spreading oak, with his huntsmen and hounds prepared for the chaise, awaiting the signal gun from the Tower to announce that he was free. At last the welcome sound reached his ear. " Ha, ha!" he cried, " the deed is done! uncouple the hounds and away." This was all the regret he expressed for the death of the woman he had pretended to love so well.

His widowhood lasted just one night, for the next morning he was at Wolf Hall, where he was united to the beautiful Jane Seymour. The ceremony was performed in the parish church, and was succeeded by a feast at which several members of the king's privy counsel were present.

Then the royal couple proceeded to Winchester, and from there to London. A grand reception was held 011 the 29th of May, when Jane was presented as queen.

When parliament met, a few days later, the lord-chan cellor made a lengthy speech setting forth the king's virtues, trying to justify his vagaries in the matrimonial line by a great deal of tedious, false reasoning, and winding up with the information that Anne Boleyn's daughter was not heir to the throne of England. Part of this speech was devoted to setting forth the noble sacrifices made by Henry VIII. for the benefit of his people.

JANE SEYMOUR.

The speaker chosen by the House of Commons went further, and loaded the king with the most fulsome compliments, comparing him to Samson, Solomon, and Absalom combined. Thus was Henry VIII. encouraged in his wickedness, until, as Cardinal Wolsey wisely said : " he actually forgot that there was both heaven and hell."

The Princess Mary was on good terms with her stepmother, who effected a reconciliation between her and the king; but the conditions were so cruel, that there was not much to be grateful for. Perhaps Jane was not responsible for them, and as we have so little that is favorable to relate of this queen, we will give her the benefit of the doubt. She made no enemies, because she avoided expressing any decided opinions, and preserved as much as possible a placid silence, and permitted herself to be governed, in all things, by her husband. If regard for her head prompted such behavior, at least she was wise.

The winter of 1537 was a remarkably cold one, and the royal couple with their entire court crossed the frozen Thames on horseback, so thick and solid was the ice.

Henry's two other queens had been crowned, so he thought the same honor ought to be conferred on the third, but the continuance of the pestilence caused that ceremony to be postponed so long that death prevented it altogether, for Jane Seymour livtd only eighteen months after her marriage. Meanwhile, she was living at Hampton Court, where her little son was born, who afterwards became Edward VI.

[A.D. 1537.] This prince was baptized at midnight, and both his sisters, Mary and Elizabeth, took part in the ceremony, which was succeeded by such a blowing of trumpets as must have been very trying, indeed, to the nerves of a young infant.

The next day Jane Seymour died. Her body was embalmed and laid on a car of state covered with a rich vel vet cloth. On top of this pall was a wax figure resembling the dead queen dressed in regal robes with a crown, sceptre, and jewels.

On the 12th of November the car was drawn by six horses to St. George's Chapel, where the corpse was interred.

Henry VIII. wrote a letter to Francis I. rejoicing over the birth of his son and expressing considerable regret at the death of his wife. He really did put on mourning attire, and appeared depressed in spirits for several weeks. This is all that could be expected of so worldly and gay a king.

4. ANNE OF CLEVES

ANNE OF CLEVES was a most unfortunate, ill-treated princess, but she possessed so many virtues that she surely deserved a better fate than to become the wife of a king so devoid of the feelings of a gentleman as Henry VIII.

After the death of his third queen, this capricious monarch did not find it so easy to get another as he probably expected it would be. Certainly it must have been a woman of rare courage who would willingly subject herself to such a yoke, knowing the experience of his other victims.

Jane Seymour had not been dead more than a month when he made a request of Francis I. that he might be permitted to choose a lady from the royal blood of France for his queen. That monarch replied, "that there was not a damsel of any degree in his own dominions who should not be at his disposal."

Henry was quite flattered at this compliment, and thought it would only be necessary for him to put out his hand to secure any woman he might condescend to favor, so he requested Francis just to bring all the fairest ladies of his court to Calais for him to take his choice. The gallantry of the French king was shocked at such an idea, and he replied, "that it was impossible to bring ladies of noble blood to market as horses are trotted out at a fair."

Then Henry wanted to marry James V.'s lady-love, whom he had seen and admired, not paying the slightest attention to the fact that she was already engaged. When he found it impossible to get her, he was ready to consider the proposition of his ambassador with regard to her sister or Mademoiselle Vendome.

"Let them be brought to Calais," he said, "and I will take a look at them."

"That would be impossible," was the reply; "but your majesty could send somebody to Paris to see them."

"Good gracious! how can I depend upon any one but myself? "asked Henry. " I must see them, and hear them sing; and what is more, I must see how they look while they are singing," he added.

By the end of the year he found that there was no hope for him in France, so he put on a most melancholy air, and pretended to be dreadfully grieved at the death of his pretty Jane.

This state of mind lasted for about two years; then Cromwell spoke in such flattering terms of the princesses of the house of Cleves that Henry began to think he had played the *role* of forlorn widower long enough.

Cromwell had only seen Sybilla, the eldest daughter of the Duke of Cleves. She was married to the Duke of Saxony, and was famed for her talents, virtues, charming manners, and extreme beauty. But unfortunately for Henry, Anne, the second daughter, was as unlike her sister as possible, and had no accomplishments whatever, with the exception of needlework.

Holbein, the celebrated Dutch artist, was required to paint the portraits of both Anne and her younger sister, Amelia, for Henry's inspection, and Christopher Mount was sent to negotiate the treaty of marriage. He wrote a letter to Cromwell filled with Anne's praises and said, "she as far excelleth the Dutchess of Saxony as the golden sun excelleth the silver moon."

The Duke of Saxony was very much opposed to a union of his sister-in-law with a man of Henry VIII.'s character, but he was the champion of the Reformation, and Christopher Mount assured him "that the cause of Protestantism in Europe would be greatly advanced by the influence of a Lutheran Queen of England, for Henry was easily managed through his wives."

The Duke of Cleves died in 1559, but his son, who succeeded him, favored Anne's marriage with King Henry, and so did their mother, both being strong allies of the Protestant cause, and feeling that even though it might be a sacrifice, it ought to be made for the sake of their religion.

One of Henry's commissioners wrote him that Anne "occupieth much of her time with her needle. She can read and write her own language, but French and Latin or other language she knoweth not; nor yet can sing or play on any instrument, for they take it here in Germany for a rebuke and an occasion of lightness that great ladies should be learned, or have any knowledge of music." He also speaks of her gentle and amiable temper, but above all he praises her sobriety, which is quite amusing.

Ever since the death of Jane Seymour the Catholics and Protestants of England had vied with each other as to which should be next represented in the queen. It was the magic brush of Hans Holbein that decided the question, and Cromwell won a triumph over Gardiner, Norfolk, and his other rivals, though it brought him ruin at last.

At length all matters of state policy and ceremony were arranged, and the young princess bade farewell to her mother, brother, and sisters, by whom she was tenderly beloved.

The first week in October, 1539, she left her native city, Dusseldorf on the Rhine, attended by a splendid escort. On her arrival at Antwerp she was received by the English merchants there, who gave her a grand torchlight procession by daylight. Next day she proceeded on her journey, and arrived at Calais December n.

About a mile outside of the town she was met by a regiment of armed men, with the king's archers, all in gay attire, besides the Earl of Southampton, Lord William Howard, and many other lords and gentlemen. Gregory Cromwell, with twenty-four others wore coats of satin damask and velvet, with gold chains of great value, and two hundred yeoman who followed them were dressed in the king's colors, red and blue cloth.

The Earl of Southampton welcomed the royal bride and conducted her into Calais, where such a peal of guns was shot from the ships on her arrival that all her retinue were astonished. Then firing began all along the coast, and was continued by the vessels until there were one hundred and fifty rounds, and so much smoke that the people in Anne's train could scarcely see each other.

The following day she was presented by the mayor with a hundred gold sovereigns, and for about three weeks after her arrival there were all sorts of pastimes and festivities. Meanwhile Henry impatiently awaited his long-expected bride, and busied himself with the execution of four worthy abbots.

The wind did not favor her progress until the 27th, when she embarked, attended by a fleet of fifty ships, and arrived at Deal the same day. The princess was received by a great company of ladies and gentlemen, and conducted to Dover Castle, where she remained until the next Monday, when, in a dreadful storm, she set out for Canterbury. Several days of travel brought the royal bride to Rochester, and New Year's Day was spent at the bishop's palace in that town.

The king was so impatient to see her, that, in company with eight of his gentlemen-in-waiting, he rode to Rochester to steal a look at his German bride, who, no doubt he thought, would rival the bright-eyed Boleyn and the fair Seymour.

On his arrival he sent a messenger to inform Anne "that he had brought her a New Year's gift, if she would please to receive it."

He followed his messenger into the room where she sat, but a glance was sufficient to show him that he had been deceived. She was by no means a pretty woman, and Henry regarded himself as an injured person in having to marry her. Perhaps she was not more charmed with his appearance or manners, but she sank upon her knees at his approach and did her best to receive him lovingly. He raised her gently, and kissed her, but there could not have been much conversation between them so long as they had to employ an interpreter. Besides her language was so displeasing to his musical ear that he did not want to hear more of it than he could help, though he knew before she came that she could speak no English. The moment he left her presence he sent for the lords who had brought her over and made his complaints.

The New Year's gift that he had provided for Anne was a muff and tippet of rich sable, but when he found she was not handsome he would not honor her by presenting it with his own hands, but sent it on the following morning by a messenger.

He returned to Greenwich in a melancholy frame of mind, and abused Cromwell for having provided him with a wife whom, with his usual brutality, he called a "great Flanders mare." Cromwell tried to put the blame on the Earl of Southampton, and said: "That when he found the princess so different from the pictures, and the reports that had been made of her, he ought to have stopped her at Calais till he had given the king notice that she was not so handsome as she had been represented." The admiral replied bluntly "that he was not invested with any such authority, his commission was to bring her to England, and he had obeyed orders." The king interrupted them by ordering them to find some means to get him out of his engagement. There was a great deal of discussion about the matter, but no objection to the marriage could be invented that would be at all satisfactory to Anne's relations in Germany, so Cromwell assured the king that as a matter of policy he must do nothing to gain the ill-will of her friends.

"Is there no remedy but that I must needs put my neck into this yoke?" exclaimed Henry, passionately.

After these gracious words, which it is to be hoped did not reach the ears of the insulted lady who was waiting his orders at Dartford, he commanded the most splendid preparations to be made for his marriage. On the 3d of January a rich tent, covered with cloth of gold, was pitched at the foot of Shooter's

Hill for the royal bride, and other tents around for her ladies. Twelve hundred gentlemen were ranged in double file from the park gates to the heath awaiting the arrival of the king with his bride. About twelve o'clock her grace came down from Shooter's Hill, accompanied by a hundred of her own nation, the Dukes of Norfolk and Suffolk, the Archbishop of Canterbury, with other bishops, lords and knights who had come from France, and went towards the tents, where Dr. Kaye, her almoner, presented all the officers and servants of her household, and addressed to her an eloquent Latin oration, of which she did not understand a word. It was answered by her brother's secretary, who acted as interpreter. Then Anne stepped out of her chariot, and was saluted and welcomed by sixty-five ladies, whom she thanked and kissed, after which all entered the tents to warm themselves, for the weather was exceedingly cold and disagreeable. When the king heard that his bride had arrived at her tent he set out through the park to meet her, accompanied by the officers of his council and his gentlemen in waiting, all richly attired in velvet coats embroidered in gold, and mounted on fine large horses. The Marquis of Dorset rode alone, attired in purple velvet and bearing the king's sword of state. Some distance behind him came Henry VIII, mounted on a splendid white courser with trappings of cloth of gold embroidered with pearls. All the buckles, bit, and pendants were of solid gold. The king wore an embroidered purple velvet coat, the sleeves and breast of which were slashed, showing cloth of gold beneath, and fastened together with large buttons of diamonds, rubies, and oriental pearls. His sword and girdle were studded with costly emeralds, and his cap was so covered with jewels that it was not possible to fix a value on it. Around his neck was a deep collar thickly studded with rubies and pearls.

When the bride was informed of Henry's approach she walked out of her tent, mounted a white horse, and, surrounded by her footmen, rode forward to meet him. Her dress was made of rich cloth of gold, cut round in Dutch fashion without a train. On her head she wore a close cap, above which was a circular bonnet ornamented with oriental pearls. Across her brow was a coronet of black velvet, and around her neck a band of superb diamonds. Henry saluted her in the most courteous manner, took off his hat and embraced her as though he really cared for her, while she, not forgetting her duty, and perhaps the instructions she had received, thanked him sweetly and praised the arrangements he had made for her reception. No doubt he was pleased with all the flattering remarks she felt obliged to make to him. Then he put her on his right side and they rode along together, he acting a deceitful part in trying to appear pleased, and she filled with indignation at the way he had scorned her.

When the grand cavalcade that followed and preceded the royal pair arrived at Greenwich Castle all the men alighted from their horses excepting the king, who rode to the inner court with his bride. When the queen had alighted from her horse Henry tenderly embraced her, and bade her "welcome to her own," then conducted her through the hall that had been prepared for her reception. There he left her and went, to his room, where he had an interview with Cromwell, to whom he made bitter complaints about the appearance of his unlucky bride.

Cromwell said he was sorry his grace was not better satisfied, whereupon Henry bade him call his council together to see whether they could not hit upon some plan for getting him out of this marriage. The council met that very afternoon, but failed to aid the king out of his dilemma, and this put him in such a bad humor that he would not say what he had determined to do until the next Monday morning; then he ordered the marriage ceremony to be performed next day, without even consulting the bride.

He wore a gown of cloth of gold, with raised silver flowers all over it. His coat was crimson satin embroidered and slashed, the points fastened with large diamonds, and a rich collar about his neck.

He entered the presence-chamber, and calling Cromwell to him, said, "My lord, if it were not to satisfy the world and my realm, I would not do what I must do this day for any earthly thing." Then one of the officers of the household informed him that the queen was ready. He advanced towards her chamber door, but had to wait several minutes before she appeared, which made him very angry. Who can blame the poor woman for her tardiness? she would have been excusable if she had refused to come at all. At last Henry sent one of his lords to bring her. She was dressed in a robe of cloth of gold, thickly embroidered in large flowers of oriental pearls. The skirt was cut, as before, round without a train, and at her neck and waist were costly jewels. Her hair fell luxuriantly over her shoulders, and on her head was a coronet of diamonds, with a few sprigs of rosemary. She walked modestly forward, between the Earls of Overstein and Essex, with a sad, demure expression, and on approaching the spot where the king stood made three low obeisances. She was followed by her ladies.

The Archbishop of Canterbury and Cranmer performed the marriage ceremony, the Earl of Overstein gave her away, and on her wedding-ring was engraved this sentence "God send me weel to keepe."

On the 4th of February the king and queen went up the Thames in grand state to their palace of Westminster. Henry kept up an outward show of attention to his bride, but she knew not the art of pleasing, felt no sympathy with his tastes, and could not gain his affection.

She knew this, but could not help it. Several times she sent for Cromwell, hoping with his advice to be more successful, but he positively refused to talk privately with her. He had reasons of his own for doing so.

On the 1st of May a company of the gallant knights at court, all dressed in white velvet with rich ornaments, had a grand tournament in honor of the recent marriage, and this was the last time Henry and Anne of Cleves ever appeared together in public.

Anne studied the English language industriously, and tried in every possible manner to please her lord, but by the end of five months she was convinced that it was hopeless.

There was a low-born, unprincipled creature at court, named Sir Thomas Wriothesley, who would have done or said anything to gain favor with his sovereign, and he kept constantly lamenting over Henry's position, and how hard it was for him to be bound to a wife whom he could not love. In this way he prepared the way for a divorce, and Henry was only too ready to avail himself of any excuse. Now his sensitive conscience began to trouble him again. This time it was on the score of religion; he could not bear to think of having a Lutheran wife. No wonder poor Anne lost patience, and in a moment of pique, told him that, "if she had not been compelled to marry him she might have fulfilled her engagement with another to whom she had promised her hand."

That was enough for him; she could scarcely have said anything that would have suited him better, and he at once set to work to make her position as unpleasant as possible. His first move was to dismiss all her foreign attendants, and supply their places with English ladies of his own selection.

By this time he was in love with the young and .beautiful Katharine Howard, niece to the Duke of Norfolk, and had decided to make her his wife as soon as he could manage it. The leaders of the Catholic party favored this union, and hoped at the same time for the downfall of their great enemy, Cromwell. They were soon to be gratified, for Henry now required a tool, who would not be guided by the nice feelings of a gentleman, for carrying out his plans. Cromwell was not such a one, and he must be put out of the way. In this reign of terror nothing was easier, and in less than a month he was arrested and shut up in the Tower.

A few days later Anne was sent to Richmond under pretense that her health required change of air, and this was the prelude to the divorce for which Henry had now grown impatient.

Archbishop Cranmer had performed the marriage ceremony, and it now became his duty to divorce the king for the third time in less than seven years. This was accomplished by unanimous consent of the clergy July 13. As the queen was a stranger to English laws and customs, she was spared the humiliation of appearing before the council.

When everything was settled, Suffolk, Southampton, and Wriothesley were appointed to go to Richmond to get the queen's consent. She was so alarmed when she saw them that before the true object of their visit could be explained to her she fell fainting to the ground. No doubt the poor woman thought she was on the point of having her head cut off. When she recovered consciousness, she was told that if she would resign her title as queen Henry would adopt her for a sister, and that she should be endowed with estates to the value of 3,000 a year. This was an immense relief, and Anne expressed her willingness to resign her honors with such alacrity that the lords were quite surprised.

When Henry heard this, and saw the paper she had signed to that effect, he could not believe that she was so ready to part with so supremely precious a person. Fearing that she might relent, he wrote to his council requesting them to have her write a letter to her brother explaining her position, and expressing her earnest desire for the divorce.

Anne then wrote her mother and brother that she was honorably treated, and felt quite cheerful and contented. She hoped that no dispute would arise between her native land and England, where she purposed spending her life, and begged them in no way to interfere, no doubt dreading that if they did so it would be visited on her head.

[A.D. 1540.] On the 28th of July, Cromwell was beheaded, and the pious, learned Doctor Barnes, who had been instrumental in bringing about the marriage, was burned at the stake.

In August Henry visited his divorced wife at Richmond, and was so well received by her that he stayed to supper and seemed in excellent humor. Two days later he publicly introduced Katharine Howard at court as his queen.

WATERLOO BRIDGE AND SOMERSET HOUSE.

In the meantime Anne passed her time very pleasantly at Richmond, dressed magnificently, and performed many deeds of charity; in short, she was happier than she had been since her departure from home.

Sixteen months later Katharine was thrown into prison, and then several attempts were made by various parties to bring about the reunion of Henry and Anne, but fortunately for her without success. From her retirement she heard of the misery the king endured when he became convinced of how his new wife had deceived him, and she must have been more than human if she did not feel somewhat gratified when the royal Bluebeard was compelled to part from her.

Katharine Howard enjoyed sixteen months of boundless influence over her husband, but her lucky star was soon to wane, and without being allowed to open her lips in her own defense save to her confessor, she was led like a sheep to the slaughter. Her execution took place February 13.

[A.D. 1577-] Anne of Cleves outlived Henry VIII and his last wife, and died during the reign of Queen Mary at the Palace of Chelsea, aged forty-one.

5. KATHARINE HOWARD

THERE is not a family in England whose name has appeared so often in its history, whether for good or for bad, as that of the Howards, nor one whose members filled such varied and important positions, as every attentive reader will admit.

Katharine Howard was nearly related to Anne Boleyn; she became the fifth wife of Henry VIII., and is by no means one of the nobler specimens of the family to which she belonged.

She was born in 1521, and had the misfortune to lose her mother while she was still young. Her father's duties called him from home a greater part of the time, and the Duchess of Norfolk, her grandmother, who had charge of Katharine, was so neglectful of her duty as to permit the child to choose her own companions, and they were unfortunately low and degraded.

Unlike most grandmothers, the duchess merely tolerated Katharine in her household, and felt that she had performed her part when the little maid was locked in her room, and the key safely deposited in her own pocket. But, like many naughty girls, Katharine managed, in spite of locks, to meet Francis Derham, one of the Duke of Norfolk's retainers, to whom she secretly engaged herself. In order to be nearer his lady-love, Derham entered the service of her grandmother as gentleman-usher. After a time the old lady began to observe certain signs of intimacy between this pair of lovers, and on entering a room one day unexpectedly she found them romping together. Shocked at the familiarity of her usher towards her granddaughter, she boxed the ears of the lady-attendant for permitting it, punished Katharine, and dismissed Derham from her service.

After that Katharine was kept under greater restraint, and as she grew into womanhood learned to behave properly, and became remarkable for her charming and graceful manners.

HEADS ON OLD LONDON BRIDGE.

She met Henry VIII the first time at a banquet given by the Bishop of Winchester to celebrate the monarch's marriage with Anne of Cleves, and afterwards at the house of Gardiner. The king took such a fancy to her that it was not long before he secured her appointment as maid-of-honor to the queen. It has been supposed that Katharine was instrumental in bringing about the death of Cromwell, but, as she only intrigued for the king's favors, it is not probable that she troubled her head about politics.

Henry VIII fell in love with her as he had done with Anne Boleyn and Jane Seymour, when they were maids-of-honor, and little Katharine was silly enough to be flattered by the marks of favor he showed her. The Duchess of Norfolk, instead of warning the girl of her danger, was foolish enough to encourage her to court the king's attention, and provided her with fine clothes to make her as attractive as possible to his majesty.

Henry was easily won, and privately married Katharine a few days after he was divorced from Anne of Cleves.

[A.D. 1540.] On the 8th of August, 1540, the new bride was introduced at Hampton Court as Queen of England. A short honeymoon was passed at Windsor, and then the royal couple made a tour through several counties, but the king had exhausted his treasury when he married his Flemish bride, so he could not honor Katharine Howard with either a coronation or a marriage festival. But he was very much in love, and lavished affection on her.

Six months of peace and happiness were enjoyed by the royal couple, Henry seldom leaving the side of his young wife, nor permitting any of his counselors to interrupt his pleasures. Katharine felt her power, and forgot what had been the fate of her predecessors. She was soon to be reminded, however, for the realm had become divided into two parties — the Catholic and Protestant, and both were strong. The Reformers fondly hoped that Anne of Cleves might be restored to her former position, and regarded Katharine in the same unfavorable light as Anne Boleyn had been looked upon by the Catholics.

At last, in the spring, came a crisis in the shape of an insurrection by the Catholics in Yorkshire, headed by Sir John Neville. Henry thought Cardinal Pole was the cause of it, and so took his revenge by ordering the execution of the Countess of Salisbury, Pole's mother, who had been in the Tower for more than a year. When the aged lady heard of it she refused to lay her head upon the block, saying, "So should traitors do, but I am none, and if you will have my head you must win it as you can." Thereupon the brutal ruffian who acted as executioner dragged her by her hoary locks, and "slovenly butchered the woman in whose veins flowed the noblest blood of England."

For the purpose of ascertaining the exact state of affairs in Yorkshire, King Henry set out with his wife for that place early in July, 1541, leaving Cranmer, Audley, and Seymour, three Protestant adherents, among his counselors at home. At Yorkshire the royal couple were met by two hundred gentlemen in velvet coats, with four thousand yeomen, who knelt while one of their number offered nine hundred pounds. At another place three hundred ecclesiastics presented six hundred pounds, and so on until Henry found himself much richer than when he started on his journey. Queen Katharine saw more of the pomp of royalty at this time than she had done during the whole year before, for the wealthy aristocracy in every part of the country vied with each other in the grandeur of their entertainments given in honor of the royal couple.

Katharine had been married little more than a year when Francis Derham returned to England, and she committed the error of appointing him as her private secretary. As soon as the king heard of the relation that had existed between this man and his wife previous to her marriage his jealousy was aroused, and the Protestant statesmen took good care to encourage every suspicion that entered their monarch's head. Meanwhile poor little Katharine was entirely unconscious of the storm that was gathering about her.

King Henry was soon forced to order her removal from Hampton Court. Wriothesley and Rich were the unprincipled, cruel agents who, determined upon the destruction of the queen, persecuted her until she was beside herself with terror and grief. Then, too, she loved her husband, and when she was compelled to leave him without one word of farewell, one look of compassion, her heart was almost broken. The king suffered also, but his council took little heed of that; it would be dangerous for them were Katharine to regain her power.

Shakespeare truly says:

Trifles, light as air,
Are to the jealous confirmations strong
As proofs of holy writ.

Katharine was removed to Sion House, and thence a few days later to the gloomy dungeon of the Tower. During the short season of terror that succeeded the queen's arrest, Derham, the poor old Duchess of Norfolk, Culpepper, Katharine's cousin, and several other persons who were guilty of no crime but that of suspecting the attachment that had existed before her marriage between Katharine and Derham, were executed.

On the 16th of January, 1542, parliament met to decide the fate of the queen, and without granting her the privilege of uttering one word in her own defense she was condemned to die. The 14th of the following month was fixed upon for the execution of this beautiful young girl, against whom no crime could be proved even through the instrumentality of the torture.

[A.D. 1542.] She met her death calmly and meekly, professing to the last her loyalty to the king. Her burial took place immediately without even the ceremonies that would have been accorded to the meanest of her subjects; she was interred in St. Peter's chapel of the Tower. When speaking of Henry VIII, Sir Walter Raleigh says: "If all the patterns of a merciless tyrant had been lost to the world they might have been found in this prince."

STAIRWAY.

6. KATHARINE PARR

KATHARINE PARR was the first Protestant Queen of England, and the only one of the wives of Henry VIII. who supported the doctrine of the Reformation with sincerity. She was an Englishwoman, but not of royal birth, being the only daughter of Sir Thomas Parr, a knight. She was gifted by nature with a fine mind, which was carefully cultivated by her excellent mother, as some of her writings that still exist certainly prove. She read and wrote Latin well, and had some knowledge of Greek.

When a little girl she never could bear to sew, and often said to her mother, "my hands are ordained to touch crowns and scepters, not spindles and needles." But Lady Parr was too wise to allow such notions to take a strong hold of her daughter's mind, and insisted on her performing those duties that befitted her station in life; consequently her embroidery, of which specimens have been preserved, shows unusual skill and industry. At Lizergh Castle a magnificent counterpane and toilet-cover are exhibited as the work of her hands, and although three centuries have passed since it was done, the colors are scarcely dimmed at all. The material is the richest white satin. In the center is a medallion of a raised eagle beneath the royal crown, surrounded by a wreath of flowers in colored silks and gold thread. At each corner is a large dragon in purple, crimson, and gold, while bouquets of flowers in gorgeous colors are dispersed here and there over the other part. The pieces match, but are of different proportions.

KATHARINE PARR.

Katharine was married twice before she became the wife of Henry VIII. Her first husband was Lord Edward Borough, a middle-aged widower with several children, who died a short time after the marriage. John Neville, Lord Latimer, was her second choice; he was also a widower with children, and Katharine's amiable temper and sound sense so well fitted her to perform the duties a stepmother that she was loved and esteemed by the families of both her husbands.

She was not more than twenty-nine years old when she was left a widow for the second time. It was then that she became a convert to the Reformed religion, and encouraged its apostles to meet daily in her chamber of state to preach their sermons.

She was not only pious, learned and handsome, but she possessed great wealth, and was connected by descent or marriage with some of the noblest families in England.

Scarcely six months had elapsed after the death of Lord Latimer when she was informed by Henry VIII that she was the lady whom he intended to honor by making her his sixth wife. She was amazed, and no doubt terrified, when she recalled the cruel treatment of her royal suitor's other victims. Besides Lord Seymour was courting her, and she had favored his attentions. But that gentleman valued his head so much that no sooner did he hear of his all-powerful royal brother-in-law's intention than he vanished from the scene, leaving Katharine to transfer her affection as best she might.

[A.D. 1543.] She exchanged her widow's weeds for bridal robes, and was married at Hampton Court without pageantry, but with all suitable observance of ceremony.

We are reminded of the fair Scheherazade in the Arabian Nights, who married the sultan, knowing that it was his custom to take a fresh wife every day and cut off her head in the morning.

But the cross, selfish old tyrant whom Katharine Parr had the courage to marry was in such bad health that he needed a skillful nurse; perhaps for that reason she felt confident that her position would be secure. On the day of her marriage she gave presents of bracelets set with rubies, as well as a liberal sum of money, to the Princesses Mary and Elizabeth.

The University of Cambridge sent the king a congratulatory letter on his choice of a Protestant wife, and the celebrated Roger Ascham corresponded with her in the name of that college, requesting her to write oftener, and not to shrink from being called learned. The dignity of the scholar and the queen are beautifully blended with the tenderness of the woman in the character of Katharine Parr after she ascended the throne.

She became an object of jealous ill-will to Gardiner, the leader of the Catholic party, who feared her influence over the king. Scarcely two weeks after the marriage he advised Henry to appoint a commission to search every house in Windsor for books written in favor of the new religion. Henry consented, but made an exception of the castle, no doubt having reason to know that more of such works would be found hidden away in his own household than in all the town put together.

The result was that many men and women were arrested, tried, and condemned to death, and although the flames of their martyrdom were kindled almost in sight of the Protestant queen, she was unable to save the victims. She knew well enough that the murder of these humble Reformers was a blow aimed at herself, and that Gardiner was playing a bold game against all those professing her religion.

One of the first acts of justice that Katharine performed after she became queen was to restore the king's two daughters, Mary and Elizabeth, to their proper position at court, after which she was constantly making them presents, and showing them many deeds of tenderness and motherly care. She and Mary were opposed to each other in religious belief, but they were about the same age, had the same accomplishments and tastes, and soon became warm and steadfast friends. Elizabeth's brilliant talents were drawn forth and encouraged by her gifted stepmother, who also directed the studies of Edward.

In one of his letters to her he says: " I thank you, most noble and excellent queen, for the letters you have lately sent me; not only for their beauty, but for their imagination. When I see your good writing and the excellence of your genius, quite surpassing my invention, I am sick of writing. But then I think how kind your nature is, and that whatever proceeds from a good, kind intention will be acceptable; and so I write you this letter."

Her celebrated work, "The Lamentations of a Sinner," is one of the finest specimens of English composition of that period. It is a treatise on morality and the imperfections of human nature.

Henry would have been miserable with a woman of such superior intellect if she had not constantly flattered him and studied his various moods. But so great was the influence she acquired over him, and the confidence he felt in her wisdom, that when he went on an expedition against France he appointed her to govern his realm as Queen Regent of England and Ireland, assisted by the Earl of Hertford.

During his absence he wrote very loving letters to his wife, who, together with her royal step-children, resided in one house.

[A.D. 1544.] She showed a great deal of moral courage, but by her beauty, tact, and domestic virtues she had made herself so necessary to her fat, dropsical husband that she was dearer to him than any of her predecessors had been.

Henry had become so unwieldy from disease that he could not move without assistance, and his wife showed herself the most patient and tender of nurses. Sometimes she would remain on her knees for hours bathing and bandaging his ulcerated leg, for he would not permit anybody to touch it but her.

[A.D. 1546.] The last occasion of festivity at the court of Henry VIII. was when ambassadors arrived to arrange terms of peace between France and England. They were met by a numerous cavalcade of nobles, knights and gentlemen, headed by the young heir to the throne, Prince Edward, who, though only in his ninth year, was mounted on a charger, and welcomed them in the most graceful and engaging manner. He conducted them to Hampton Court, where for ten days they were feasted and entertained with great magnificence by the king and queen.

Henry presented Katharine with jewels of great value, that she might make a good appearance before their French guests, he also provided new and costly hangings and furniture for her apartments as well as a quantity of handsome silver.

Wriothesley and Bishop Gardiner were alarmed at Katharine's ever-increasing influence, not only over her husband, but over the mind of young Edward as well, and watched her closely, in the hope that they might be able to make some charge against her. Nothing offered itself excepting her religious opinions, which were opposed to Henry's.

Several persons were burned to death about this time for professing the reformed doctrine, among whom was the young, beautiful and learned Anne Askew. She was a lady of honorable birth, who became a convert to the new faith, and was for that reason violently driven from her home by her cruel husband. Resuming her maiden name, she worked hard for her religion, and was aided by the first ladies at court. When it was discovered that she had sent books to the queen, she was singled out as a victim by those who hoped by means of torture to wring some confession from her by which Katharine might be charged with heresy or treason. But they were mistaken, for the heroic Anne Askew died at the stake like a true martyr, "with an angelic expression on her smiling countenance."

Sir George Blagge was arrested also, but he happened to be one of the king's prime favorites, and was sometimes called by the endearing nickname of "pig." As soon as Henry heard of this arrest he sent for Wriothesley and rated him well, commanding him to draw up a pardon on the spot. On his release Blagge flew to thank his preserver, who on seeing him cried out, "Ah! my pig, are you here safe again!" "Yes, sire," was the reply, "and if your majesty had not been better than your bishops your pig had been roasted ere this time."

OLD ST. PAUL'S.

The next attack was on the queen herself, whom Wriothesley and Gardiner had resolved to strike with a fatal blow. They told the king that her sister, Lady Herbert, not only read the books that he had prohibited, but also gave them to Katharine to read. Now it happened that the royal couple often conversed on theological subjects in their hours of domestic privacy, and Henry enjoyed his wife's ready wit and eloquence. She courted these subjects, because, knowing that he was suffering from an incurable malady, she felt it her duty to turn his mind heavenward.

One day in the presence of Gardiner she went a little too far in opposing her lord's views, and as he was suffering with his leg he felt rather more irritable than usual. He therefore snappishly put a stop to the discussion; after making a few pleasant remarks Katharine left the room. "A good hearing it is," said Henry sharply, "when women become such clerks; and much to my comfort to come, in mine old age, to be taught by my wife!" Gardiner took advantage of the king's wounded vanity to insinuate things against his wife that he would not have dared to say a few days before. He flattered him on his knowledge of theology, and declared that his majesty excelled the princes of that age and every other, as well as all the professed doctors of divinity, so much that it was absurd for anybody to think of arguing with him as the queen had just done. He added that it was painful for any of his counselors to hear it, because those who were so bold in words would not hesitate to commit any act of disobedience. In fact he so poisoned the king's mind as to gain from him a warrant to consult with others of his party about drawing up articles against the queen that might bring her head to the block. But they decided to begin with the ladies of the court whom she esteemed most, and to search their trunks and closets for something to charge Katharine with, and after they had found it to arrest her in the middle of the night and take her in a barge to the Tower.

All this time the queen suspected nothing, but continued her nursing of her husband and her religious discussions with him as before. One day an attendant of Katharine's picked up a paper in the gallery of Whitehall that Wriothesley had dropped. It contained a list of charges against the queen with an order for her arrest, and bore Henry's signature. The queen was devastated and immediately in fear for her life.

Katharine went to the king's rooms and there he immediately began to discuss religion with her, in particular contradicting many of her reformist beliefs. Recognizing the test, Katharine agreed with it all, telling Henry that 'women by their first creation were made subject to men' and that 'men out to instruct their wives, who would do all their learning from them'. The king was 'a prince of such excellent learning and wisdom' that she would gladly follow his counsel. But this appeal to Henry's vanity was not enough. 'You are become a doctor able to instruct us and not to be instructed by us,' the king said, referring to her earlier lecture. But Katharine replied that he had 'much mistaken the freedom she had taken to argue with him', for she had only done it to learn from him and distract him from his illness. 'And is it even so?' asked Henry, with a smile. 'Then Kate, we are friends again.' Katharine Parr had escaped.

But no one had told the king's council. When Wriothesley and forty guards arrived to arrest Katharine the next day, the king himself beat them about the heads and shoulders, calling them foul names. Katharine was thus saved in a most public and spectacular fashion, and was soon gifted with more jewels and plate than before.

Her appeal to Henry's vanity saved her life and it also allowed the king to remind everyone who was the real master. Wriothesley had sought to recreate the destruction of Wolsey and Cromwell, using the king's temper to destroy his personal enemies. But Henry VIII was of a mind to do otherwise. He had long lamented the loss of Cromwell and he disliked any manipulation by his counselors. By saving Katharine in such a public manner, he forced his courtiers to recognize his omnipotence and mutability.

But he was not indestructible. The king's health began a decline in the spring of 1546 from which he only sporadically recovered. By the winter, he was dangerously ill. Katharine's own position gained new prominence since upon Henry's death she would be the dowager queen. She already had great influence over her stepson Prince Edward. She continued to nurse Henry assiduously, but was sent away to Greenwich Palace with Mary and Elizabeth for Christmas celebrations. She returned to London on 10 January but never saw the king again. Henry VIII died in the early morning hours of 28 January 1547.

After Henry's death, Thomas Seymour's elder brother Edward assumed the title Protector of the Kingdom, ruling in the name of his nine year old nephew. Katharine, meanwhile, married Thomas with what others (including her royal stepchildren) felt was indecent haste. The actual date is not known but Seymour referred to himself as her husband in a letter of 17 May. The wedding took place in the moonlit gardens of Chelsea Manor. Letters indicate that the ambitious Seymour pressed for a quick union. As a dowager queen, Katharine was expected to behave perfectly; also, it was theoretically possible she was pregnant by Henry VIII. For once, the always dutiful Katharine had acted impulsively. She had given up Thomas Seymour once and would not do so again.

For the new king's counselors, the marriage was a disaster. They recognized Seymour's ambition even as Katharine fell even more deeply in love. Edward Seymour's wife Anne Stanhope, now the duchess of Somerset, engaged in a petty battle of precedence with Katharine. Also, there were arguments over Katharine's possessions, particularly jewelry which Henry VIII had given her. Still, there was far happier news to distract her. In late November 1547, thirty-five years old and childless through three previous marriages, Katharine Parr became pregnant.

However, her pregnancy was not the happy triumph she had expected. Her husband proved too forward with the young Princess Elizabeth and Katharine was forced to send her step-daughter away. This breach hurt them both deeply. The young Lady Jane Grey remained with the household, however, for Seymour had 'bought' her from her ambitious parents, hoping to marry her to Prince Edward.

Katharine gave birth to a girl named Mary at Sudeley Castle in Gloucestershire on 30 August. Jane Grey stood as godmother to the infant, but the happy occasion took a quick turn for the worse. Katharine Parr soon fell victim to puerperal sepsis, or 'childbed fever', which had also killed Queen Jane Seymour. She suffered painful delusions before sinking into calm, able to dictate her will and final wishes. She died on 5 September, and Jane Grey acted as chief mourner at the funeral. She was buried at Sudeley in St Mary's Church.

Katharine's Parr life was always one of duty and kindness. She left behind a formidable tradition of scholarship and religious devotion, as evidenced by her own books. The great tragedy of her life was that, when finally able to marry for love, her happiness was all too brief.

7. SUMMARY AND CONCLUSION

The wives of Henry VIII were the six queens consort married to Henry VIII of England between 1509 and 1547.

The six wives (queens consort) of King Henry VIII were, in order: Catherine of Aragon (annulled), Anne Boleyn (annulled then beheaded), Jane Seymour (died, childbed fever), Anne of Cleves (annulled), Catherine Howard (annulled then beheaded), and Catherine Parr (survived). Because annulment legally voids a marriage, technically speaking Henry would have said he had only 2 "wives", but his marriage to Queen Catherine of Aragon was declared legal and valid during the reign of his daughter Queen Mary I.

It is often noted that Catherine Parr "survived him"; in fact Anne of Cleves also survived the king and was the last of his queens to die. Of the six queens, Catherine of Aragon, Anne Boleyn and Jane Seymour each gave Henry one child who survived infancy—two daughters and one son, all three of whom would eventually accede to the throne. They were Queen Mary I, Queen Elizabeth I, and King Edward VI.

Catherine Howard and Anne Boleyn, Henry's two queens that were beheaded, were first cousins. Several of his wives worked in at least one of his other wives' service. Anne Boleyn worked in Catherine of Aragon's service; Jane Seymour worked in Catherine of Aragon's and Anne Boleyn's service; and Catherine Howard worked in Anne of Cleves's.

Henry was distantly related to all six of his wives through their mutual ancestor, King Edward I of England.

Henry and at least four of his wives (Catherine of Aragon, Anne Boleyn, Jane Seymour and Catherine Parr) have been characters in opera (for details, see List of historical opera characters).

Catherine of Aragon

Catherine of Aragon (1485–1536) was Henry's first wife. After the death of Arthur, her first husband and Henry's brother, a papal dispensation was obtained to enable her to marry Henry, though the marriage did not take place until after he came to the throne in 1509. Catherine bore him a daughter in 1516, Mary I, but no sons survived past infancy, due to miscarriages and stillbirths. It is said that Henry truly loved Catherine of Aragon, he himself professed it many a time in song, letters, inscriptions, public declarations etc.

Henry, at the time a Roman Catholic, sought the Pope's approval for an annulment on the grounds that his marriage was invalid because Catherine had first been his brother's wife. Henry had begun an affair with Anne Boleyn, who is said to have refused to become his mistress (Henry had already consummated an affair with and then dismissed Anne's sister, Mary Boleyn, and Anne wanted to avoid the same treatment).

Despite the pope's refusal, Henry separated from Catherine in 1531. In the face of the Pope's continuing refusal to annul his marriage to Catherine, Henry ordered the highest church official in England, Thomas Cranmer, Archbishop of Canterbury, to convene a court to rule on the status of his marriage to Catherine. On 23 May 1533 Cranmer ruled the marriage to Catherine null and void. On 28 May 1533 he pronounced the King legally married to Anne Boleyn (with whom Henry had already secretly exchanged wedding vows, probably in late January 1533). This led to the break from the Roman Catholic Church and the later establishment of the Church of England. Shakespeare called her "The Queen of Earthly Queens".

Anne Boleyn

Anne Boleyn (1501–1536) was the second wife of Henry
VIII of England and the mother of Elizabeth I of England.
Henry's marriage to Anne, and her subsequent execution, made
her a key figure in the political and religious upheaval that was
the start of the English Reformation. The daughter of Sir
Thomas Boleyn and his wife, Lady Elizabeth Boleyn (born
Lady Elizabeth Howard), Anne was of nobler birth than Jane
Seymour; Henry's later wife. She was educated in Europe,
largely as a lady-in-waiting. She returned to France in 1532

Anne resisted the King's attempts to seduce her and she
refused to become his mistress, as her sister, Mary Boleyn, had
done. It soon became the one absorbing object of the King's
desires to secure a divorce from his wife, Catherine of Aragon,
so he could marry Anne. When it became clear that Pope
Clement VII was unlikely to give the king an annulment, the
breaking of the power of the Roman Catholic Church in
England began.

Henry had Thomas Wolsey dismissed from public office
and later had the Boleyn family's chaplain, Thomas Cranmer,
appointed Archbishop of Canterbury. In 1533, Henry and Anne
went through a secret wedding service. She soon became
pregnant and there was a second wedding service, which took
place in London on 25 January 1533. On 23 May 1533,
Cranmer declared the marriage of Henry and Catherine null and
void. Five days later, Cranmer declared the marriage of Henry
and Anne to be good and valid. Soon after, the Pope launched
sentences of excommunication against the King and the
Archbishop. As a result of Anne's marriage to the King, the
Church of England was forced to break with Rome and was
brought under the king's control. Anne was crowned Queen
Consort of England on 1 June 1533. Later that year, on 7
September, Anne bore Henry another daughter, Elizabeth.
When Anne failed to quickly produce a male heir, her only son

being stillborn, the King grew tired of her and a plot was hatched by Thomas Cromwell to execute her.

Although the evidence against her was unconvincing, Anne was beheaded on charges of adultery, incest, and high treason on 19 May 1536. Following her daughter Elizabeth's coronation as queen, Anne was venerated as a martyr and heroine of the English Reformation, particularly through the works of John Foxe. Over the centuries, Anne has inspired or been mentioned in numerous artistic and cultural works. Due to this fact, she has remained in the popular memory and Anne has been called "the most influential and important queen consort England has ever had."

Jane Seymour

Jane Seymour (1508–1537) was Henry's third wife. He first became attracted to her when he stayed with the Seymour family in September of 1535. She was one of Anne Boleyn's ladies-in-waiting and it is popularly believed she is the reason he disposed of Anne. After their marriage in 1536, she gave him his only male heir, later Edward VI. She died of postnatal complications less than two weeks after Edward's birth. Most historians believe she was Henry's favorite wife.

Anne of Cleves

Anne of Cleves was Henry's fourth wife, though they were married for only six months in 1540, from 6 January to 9 July. Anne of Cleves was a German princess. Her pre-contract of marriage with Francis I, Duke of Lorraine, was cited as grounds for an annulment. Anne agreed to this, claiming that the marriage had not been consummated, and she was given a generous settlement, including Hever Castle, former home of Henry's former in-laws, the Boleyns. She was given the name

"The King's Sister", and became a friend to him and his children. She outlived both the King and his last two wives.

Catherine Howard

Catherine Howard (1520–1542), sometimes known as "the rose without a thorn", was Henry's fifth wife. Henry was informed of her alleged adultery on 1 November 1541. After being deprived of the title of Queen, she was beheaded at the Tower of London. The night before, Catherine spent hours practicing how to lay her head upon the block, and her last words were for mercy for her family and prayers for her soul. Catherine was a first cousin of Anne Boleyn.

Catherine Parr

Catherine Parr (1512–1548), was the sixth and last wife of Henry VIII. She was the daughter of Sir Thomas Parr of Kendal and his wife Lady Maud Greene. Through her father, Catherine Parr was a direct descendant of King Edward III of England (House of Plantagenet) and Philippa of Hainault, Queen Consort of England through their son Prince John of Gaunt, 1st Duke of Lancaster Plantagenet and his mistress, later wife, Katherine Swynford née Roët; thus making her ancestors part of the House of Lancaster. Through John of Gaunt's daughter Lady Joan Beaufort, Countess of Westmoreland (the maternal great-great grandmother of Henry) Catherine was a 3rd cousin, once removed of her husband, Henry VIII. This same Lady Joan Beaufort came from the illegitimate Beaufort line of John of Gaunt Plantagenet and his mistress at the time, Lady Katherine de Swynford.

Following Gaunt's marriage to Katherine in 1396, their children (the Beauforts) were legitimized. Lady Margaret Beaufort, mother of Henry VII, was the grandniece of Lady Joan Beaufort. Through this relation, Catherine was also a 4th cousin, once removed of Henry VIII on his paternal side. It was through Margaret's line that her descendants had a strong claim to the throne and after the Battle of Bosworth Field on 22 August 1485, her only son Henry, became King Henry VII of England. His claim to the throne was that he was the last reasonably legitimate male descendant of Edward III. Thus through him the Tudor dynasty rose to power.

Catherine Parr showed herself to be the re-newer of Henry's court as a family home for his children. Catherine was determined to present the royal household as a close-knit one in order to demonstrate strength through unity to Henry's opposers. Perhaps Catherine's most significant achievement was Henry's passing of an act that confirmed both Princess Mary's and Elizabeth's line in succession for the throne, despite the fact that they had both been made illegitimate by divorce or remarriage. Such was Henry's trust in Catherine that he chose her to rule as Regent while he was attending to the War in France and in the unlikely event of the loss of his life, she was to rule as Regent until six year old Edward came of age. This was a very singular indication of Henry's trust and love for Catherine.

Catherine also has a special place in history as she was the most married queen of England, having had four husbands in all; Henry was her third spouse. She had been widowed three times in rapid succession. After Henry's death, she married Thomas Seymour, uncle of Edward VI, to whom she had formed an attachment prior to her marriage with Henry. She had one child by Seymour, Mary, and died in childbirth. Mary's history is unknown, but she is believed to have died as a toddler.

Parr was probably named after Henry's first wife, Catherine of Aragon.

Mistresses of Henry VIII

Henry VIII also had several mistresses during his marriages. While married to Catherine of Aragon, he had a relationship with Bessie Blount, which lasted around eight years; his friend's wife, Elizabeth Carew; Etiennette de la Baume; Anne Hastings, Countess of Huntingdon; Elizabeth Amadas; and most notably with Mary Boleyn, the sister of his second wife Anne.

During his marriage to Anne, he had a relationship with an unnamed lady, followed by a six-month affair with the Queen's cousin, Mary Shelton , and most likely more unnamed women, before starting a relationship with Jane Seymour. There were also rumours about his relationships with several other women during various marriages, including the notorious Elizabeth Wyatt; Anne Bassett; Katherine Willoughby, Duchess of Suffolk; and his own son's widow, Mary Howard, Duchess of Richmond and Somerset.

The Six Wives of Henry VIII

Made in United States
Orlando, FL
03 December 2022

25417369R00054